WHAT
DO
I
KNOW?

MICHEL DE MONTAIGNE (1533–1592) was born on his family estate in Aquitaine, not far from Bordeaux. Given a classical education following Renaissance humanist principles, Montaigne was raised to speak Latin and did not learn French until he was six years old. He continued his schooling at the College of Guienne before studying law in Toulouse and embarking on a distinguished career in public service, first as a counselor of court in Périgueux and Bordeaux, then as a courtier to Charles IX. Montaigne married Françoide de la Cassaigne in 1565, with whom he had six daughters, five of whom died in infancy. After the death of his father, Montaigne returned to his family estate and retired from public life. He made the Tower of the château into a library, his 'citadel', where he isolated himself from social and family life in order to read and write.

Between 1571 and 1580 he composed the first two books of his great Essays, which were initially published in Bordeaux in 1580; Book III was only included in the fifth edition, published in 1588. Declaring 'I myself am the subject of my book', Montaigne pioneered the literary form of the essay in intellectually probing, self-reflective explorations of his inner self and the wider world. The Essays have influenced innumerable writers, including William Shakespeare, Lord Byron, Friedrich Nietzsche, Ralph Waldo Emerson and Virginia Woolf.

DAVID COWARD is Emeritus Professor of French at the University of Leeds and a translator of many books from the French, including Georges Simenon's Inspector Maigret series and Arthur Cohen's Belle du Seigneur, for which he was awarded a Scott Moncrieff Prize.

YIYUN LI is the author of seven works of fiction—The Book of Goose, Must I Go, Where Reasons End, Kinder Than Solitude, A Thousand Years of Good Prayers, The Vagrants, and Gold Boy, Emerald Girl—and the memoir Dear Friend, from My Life I Write to You in Your Life. She is the recipient of many awards, including the PEN/Malamud Award, the PEN/Hemingway Award, the PEN/Jean Stein Book Award, a MacArthur Fellowship, and a Windham-Campbell Prize. Her work has also appeared in the New Yorker, A Public Space, The Best American Short Stories, and The PEN/O. Henry Prize Stories, among other publications. She teaches at Princeton University.

MICHEL DE MONTAIGNE

WHAT
DO
I
KNOW?

ESSENTIAL ESSAYS

TRANSLATED FROM THE FRENCH
BY DAVID COWARD

WITH AN INTRODUCTION
BY YIYUN LI

PUSHKIN PRESS

Pushkin Press
Somerset House, Strand
London WC2R 1LA

The first two books of Michel de Montaigne's *Essays* were initially published
in France in 1580; a revised edition featuring a third book was published in
1588; an edition with further revisions was published posthumously in 1595

This collection first published by Pushkin Press in 2023

1 3 5 7 9 8 6 4 2

ISBN 13: 978-1-78227-881-8

Designed and typeset by Tetragon, London
Printed and bound by Clays Ltd, Elcograf S.p.A.

www.pushkinpress.com

CONTENTS

Introduction   7

To the Reader   13

PART ONE: MONTAIGNE ON MONTAIGNE

1   *On Sorrow*   17
2   *On How Our Actions Are to Be Judged by the Intention*   23
3   *On Idling*   26
4   *On Liars*   28
5   *That We Should Not Be Considered Happy Until We Are Dead*   37

PART TWO: ON THE PURSUIT OF REASON

6   *On Fear*   45
7   *To Tell True from False, It Is Folly to Rely on Our Own
    Capacities*   50
8   *On How We Can Cry and Laugh at the Same Thing*   57
9   *On Solitude*   63
10 *On the Uncertainty of Our Judgement*   83
11 *On Drunkenness*   94

PART THREE: ON GOVERNANCE AND GOVERNORS

12	On Cannibals	113
13	On the Inequality That Exists Between Us	134
14	On Sleep	151
15	On Our Lease of Life	155
16	On Carriages	160

Introduction

I became a dedicated reader of Montaigne in 2005. I was new to writing then, and relatively new to motherhood, with a three-year-old and a newborn, and about to publish my first book. For the next ten years or so, I would be reading Montaigne every day, sometimes only for ten minutes, and later, when my children were older, for thirty minutes to an hour in the afternoon, before I picked them up from school. I might not have understood the significance of this routine at the time, other than that it was a brief reprieve from a life overcrowded with the responsibilities of being a mother, a wife, a writer, and a professor.

I found Montaigne among the best conversational partners one could dream of: always available, often entertaining, never predictable. That he was knowledgeable meant that I learned something new anytime I opened his book; that his thinking meandered but with an innate logic demanded that I read with an active mind instead of being a passive recipient; and best of all, he was not writing to converse with me (or any reader) but with himself. About himself. 'Reader, I myself am the subject of my book,' stated Montaigne in his introduction to his work. 'There is no reason why you should devote your leisure time on so trivial and unprofitable a topic.'

Rightly so! And there is no reason why one should not defect from the pressing (and sometimes profitable) tasks of everyday life and dwell on a more pressing (and definitely less profitable) subject: selfhood. There are many ways to elaborate on Montaigne's work. For me, his work serves as a reminder, a prompt, even, a mandate: a regular meditation on selfhood, like daily yoga, is a healthy habit.

But what is selfhood? The question requires one to ponder over a few related questions. What is the opposite of selfhood: unselfhood or otherhood? Where is the boundary of selfhood: is it defined by time or space? And what is the right amount of attention one should pay to selfhood—that is, if there is a way to measure—without running into the risk of straying into the quagmire of egohood?

I've been pondering over these questions while reading this sleek volume of Montaigne, newly translated by David Coward and published under the title: *What Do I Know? Essential Essays*. What do I know—*Que sçay-je* or *Que sais-je* in modern French—was a sentiment known to Montaigne, which these days people use jestingly and colloquially. I do often wish for two things: that people would ask themselves the question, *what do I know*, before opining, and that people would give a thoughtful answer, instead of using it as a witty remark.

What do I know about Montaigne? A little, as a lay reader of his work. It was nearly three years into a global pandemic, and seven years since I last read Montaigne. My immediate reaction, while immersing myself in the familiar words rendered anew by this translation, was happiness; bliss, even. If this sounds preposterous, it's the preposterousness for which one is willing to endure misunderstanding and ridicule.

Writers worth rereading are those whose minds both sustain and surprise us. What a great moment, when, a few pages in, I encountered this line: 'the places I see again and books I reread smile on me by seeming fresh and new.' (On Liars, p. 31)

The longer one lives, the more places one has accumulated which one will never revisit. For instance, the army camp in central China where I spent a year between age eighteen and nineteen: there, once, during a night exercise, I hid in an abandoned ditch, shooting blank ammunitions at my comrades who played my enemies, while around me thousands of fireflies twinkled. Or, a hospital corridor leading to the morgue in Beijing, where the crowd, murmuring with curiosity and sympathy, parted as I followed my father on a gurney, which was elaborately adorned for afterlife.

And yet the longer one lives, the more reliable is the frame offered by those rereadable writers, whose words anchor our own thinking. Indeed, Montaigne's words have smiled on me this time, not only by seeming fresh and new after my sojourn from his work, but also by reminding me that by now I've known a little better where and how I can locate my selfhood. Dare I say I've become a better reader of his work?

'The mind that has no firm anchor point is lost for, as is commonly said, it is nowhere if it is everywhere.' (On Idling, p. 27) It occurs to me that the happiness I feel while rereading Montaigne has little to do with any worldly matter but a sense of knowing where I am: I am not at that dreaded place called nowhere, nor am I—nor do I aspire to be—at that illusory place called everywhere.

Nowhere-ness: I don't think I'm alone in having now and then been trapped by the feeling of being nowhere; the world seems to have experienced a collective version of that during the pandemic. Being nowhere is different from being lost. The latter implies an opposite state of existence, of being unlost, of being found again. Being nowhere, however, feels bleaker: the past and the future merge into an everlasting present, and the present is where time and space, both unchangeable, take on a permanent stillness.

Sometimes the feeling of nowhere-ness calls for the ambition of everywhere-ness. Incidentally, ambition, from its etymology, has a lot to do with everywhere-ness. According to the OED, ambition comes from Latin ambitiōn-, ambitiō, soliciting of votes, canvassing, striving after popularity, desire for advancement, ostentation, pomp; ambit-, past participial stem of ambīre, to go round or about. (Sharing this etymology are two other words: 'ambient' and 'ambience.') In our contemporary world, this ambition to be everywhere is assisted and exacerbated by technology—faster, more connected, more ubiquitous. People on social media travel to many countries, dine at different restaurants, read three hundred books a year. And yet: 'He who lives everywhere, lives nowhere,' wrote Montaigne. (On Idling, p. 27) Perhaps as a collective, we dwellers in today's world, pressed by the need to be everywhere, easily slip into nowhere.

Between nowhere and everywhere: somewhere. This time, rereading Montaigne, my intense happiness comes from knowing where I am in life. It's not an ideal or a perfect place, but a place that I accept as mine: I'm a more experienced writer since my first encounter with Montaigne; I've known sorrows in many forms, including the loss of a child; I have accumulated a handful of writers to whom I return regularly, just as the roses in my garden return to blossoming every year. I am somewhere.

Montaigne will always be among the writers I reread. His words provide one of the best anchors for one's everchanging mind. While comparing the new translation with other editions on my shelf, I noticed underlining by a blue ballpoint pen in a 1958 Penguin Classics edition. The book had been brought by a friend who had visited me in a psych ward near New York City where I, entrapped by the bleakest nowhere-ness, stayed for three weeks. (The pens given out to the patients were ballpoint pen fillings wrapped up in paper—cheap, and the least dangerous.) But I see now, rereading the annotations done in the hospital, that even then I was somewhere—I might not have known my own mind, but I trusted Montaigne's words and saved some of my memories between his lines. There are other editions, read at different times. A 1947 edition, translated by Charles Cotton and selected and illustrated by Salvador Dalí, boasts not only Montaigne's wisdoms but also Dalí's whimsies: a cluster of grapes, each a happy skull; naked bodies (or, are they naked souls?) in deep conversation; headless warriors embracing each other. The edition of Complete Essays translated by Donald M. Frame has superscript letters [ABC] in the text, indicating the work done at different times: Montaigne had returned to the same subjects at several stages of his life. Reading that edition always gives me a concrete sense of how Montaigne's mind changed over time and yet remained, or became more of, Montaigne's mind.

This new translation, a fine introduction for readers who are just about to discover Montaigne and a reliable companion for returning readers, will surely move the reader—not to nowhere, not to everywhere—but to somewhere. This somewhere-ness is perhaps the closest as I can define as selfhood.

YIYUN LI

To the Reader

This, Reader, is a book written entirely in honest good faith. From the start, it forewarns you that in it I have no purpose other than to interest kin and self. I have not set out to flatter your notion of things and have given no thought to my reputation. Such ambitions are beyond my powers. I dedicate my book to the particular use of my family and friends so that, having lost me (as they shall in the near future), they will be able to recover some few evidences of my character and moods, and that in this way they might acquire a fuller and clearer understanding of me. If my purpose had been to seek the world's favour, I should have appeared in borrowed plumes and followed a more orderly scheme of exposition. But I wish to be seen in my simple, natural and ordinary character, with no axe to grind and without artifice: for here I paint myself. My faults will show up bright in these pages as will my artless nature, insofar as respect for social conventions allows. Had I lived my life among the nations which are said still to enjoy the freedom of nature's primitive laws, I assure you that I should readily have drawn myself, whole and bare naked.

Therefore, Reader, I myself am the subject of my book. This being so, there is no reason why you should devote your leisure time to so trivial and unprofitable a topic.

And so farewell.

At Montaigne, this first day of March, one thousand five hundred and eighty.

PART ONE

Montaigne on Montaigne

Montaigne declared himself to be the subject of his book, his main purpose being to follow the injunction inscribed over the entrance to the Oracle of Apollo at Delphi: 'Know Thyself'. His thoughts were rooted in this clear-sighted estimate of the strengths and limitations of his mind and emotions. While his personality permeates his ideas, there are times when he slipped into self-examination by providing more direct 'evidences' of his characters and moods, revealing more clearly his engaging personality.

I

On Sorrow

I am one of those people who are little affected by an emotion for which I have little patience or regard, although most people, apparently by some common accord, have chosen to honour it by presenting it in a most favourable light. They dress it up as inner strength, courage and tender conscience—such a foolish, monstrous idea! More fittingly, the Italians have found another word for it: *tristezza*, a kind of heaviness of heart. For it is always a harmful state of mind, invariably irrational and unfailingly cowardly and base—an emotion in which the Stoics consistently forbid their faithful to indulge.

But when, so the story goes, Psammenitus, King of Egypt, having been defeated and made prisoner by Cambyses, King of Persia, saw his daughter walk by dressed as a serving-girl sent to fetch water from the well, and all his friends began weeping and lamenting around him, he sat quietly by, saying not a word, with his eyes fixed upon the ground. And when by and by he saw his son being led away to his death, he maintained the same composure. But on observing one of his household being led away among the captives, he began to beat his breast and fell into a state of deep grief.

This could well be said to resemble what was lately observed in one of our Princes who, being then in Trento, received word of the death of his older brother, who was the prop and honour of all his family and, then, soon after, of the demise of a younger brother, his second great hope. Having borne both these blows with exemplary fortitude, it so happened that a few days later one of his courtiers died, upon which new misfortune he was quite overcome and, abandoning his self-possession, surrendered to grief and sorrow in such a manner that those around him could only conclude that he had been affected by this final blow alone. But in truth it was because he was full to overflowing with grief that the final drop burst the dam of his self-possession.

Now it could be (say I) that we might explain the story that way if it did not go on to tell how Cambyses asked Psammenitus why he had not been moved by the fate of his son and daughter but had reacted so violently to that of one of his household.

'Because,' said he, 'only the final blow could be conveyed by tears, the first two having run so deep they were beyond expression.'

Pertinent here, perhaps, is the discovery of a painter of old who was charged with depicting Iphigenia sacrificed and, one by one, the grief of those present according to the reactions of each to the death of that beautiful young woman. By the time he came to her father, having exhausted all the expedients of his art, he painted him with features hidden as if to say that there was no visage capable of portraying grief so deep. That is why poets make believe that the wretched Niobe, having first lost seven sons and then as many daughters, being weighed down with her losses, was finally turned to stone, 'being overcome with misery' (Ovid, *Metamorphoses* VI, 304), this being their best way of rendering that bleak, unspoken, unheeding stupor which numbs our senses when the accidents of life strike with a force that exceeds the limits of what we can bear.

Such is the impact of these blows which, when they are extreme, overwhelm the mind and rob it of its freedom of expression. When we too are shaken to the core by some truly dreadful piece of news, we are stunned, numb, as if impeded in all our motions so that when afterwards the mind finds release in tears and weeping, it seems to become detached or disconnected and allows itself greater room for action and, now at its ease, 'its pain allows utterance to its voice' (Virgil, *Æneid*, XI, 151).

During the war which King Ferdinand waged against the widow of John, King of Hungary, in the environs of Buda, Raïsciac, a German captain, seeing the body being brought back of a knight who all had observed acquitting himself with great gallantry in the thick of battle, offered the conventional condolences. As curious as the others to know the identity of the man, he discovered after the armour was removed that the man was his son. But alone among the general weeping and wailing, he stood ramrod straight, speaking not a word, shedding not a tear, his eyes unwaveringly fixed upon him, until the intensity of his distress congealed his vital spirits and he fell stone dead upon the ground.

And yet, though

whoever says he burns with love scarce burns at all,

—PETRARCH, *CANZONIERE*, 170

lovers who seek to portray a love too great to bear will say:

I am lost! My senses are all stripped from me!
Lesbia! I see you and my soul, my voice do both flee away,
My body burns with an insubstantial flame,
My ears are full of their own clangour
And upon my eyes twice-fold night falls.

—CATULLUS, LI, 5

Thus it is not in the heat of the moment of intense ardour that we are capable of giving voice to our amorous complaints and feelings; at that moment, our whole being is given over to deep purposes and our body overwhelmed and aching with desire.

Yet at times from that high pitch may proceed that accidental, untimely failure of performance which so disconcerts lovers, and a loosening of the powerful grip of intense potency on the very brink of enjoyment (an accident not unknown to me). Passions which can be savoured and digested are not true passions at all.

Small griefs can speak but an aching heart is dumb.

—Seneca, Hippolytus, II, iii

An unexpected pleasure may come upon us in the same way.

When she saw me and the armaments of Troy all around, she panicked and, terror-struck, eyes staring and bloodless-cheeked, she fainted away; her voice did not return to her until long after.

—Virgil, Æneid, III, 306

In addition to the Roman woman who died surprised by joy on seeing her son return along the road from the battle at Cannæ, Sophocles and Dionysius of Syracuse who both expired rejoicing, and Talva who died in Corsica as he read the honours which the Senate in Rome had conferred upon him, we have in our own century Pope Leo X who, having been informed of the taking of Milan which he had devoutly wished for, was overcome by such excess of delight that he fell prey to a fever to which he promptly succumbed. And for a more notable example still of the follies of human nature, it is recorded by the ancients that Diodorus the Dialectician dropped dead, laid low by an extreme fit of mortification because in his academy and in front of his public, he had failed to find a way of countering an argument that had been put up against him.

I myself am not at all given to such extravagant combustibility for I am naturally hard-headed and, by the daily use and discourse of reason, make my head harder every day.

2

On How Our Actions
Are to Be Judged by the Intention

I t is said that death cancels all obligations. I know of some
who have put a very different interpretation on this notion.
Henry VII, King of England, came to an agreement with Don
Philip, son of Maximilian the emperor or, to present him
more honourably, father of the emperor Charles V: that the
said Phillip should give into his keeping his enemy the Duke
of Suffolk (of the White Rose, who had escaped and fled to
the Low Countries) against an undertaking that Henry would
make no attempt on the duke's life. Yet on his deathbed, in
his will, the king ordered his son to have the duke killed
immediately after he himself was dead.

More recently in Brussels, the tragedy of the execution of
Counts Egmont and Horn staged for us by the Duke of Alba
was remarkable for a number of extraordinary particulars.
Among them was the fact that the said Count of Egmont (on

whose word and assurance Count Horn had come to give himself up to the Duke of Alba) requested most insistently that he should be put to death first, for that way his dying would free him of the obligation to Count Horn.

Now it seems to me that death did not cancel the word Henry had given, but that even before he met his end, Count Egmont was fully released from his pledge.

For we cannot be held to account beyond the limits of what our strength and capacities can perform. It follows that actions and their consequences are not ours to command and that in reality we are in charge of nothing but our will. Therefore, and inescapably, it is in our will that all the rules and the whole duty of man begin and are rooted. This is why Count Egmont, believing both his soul and his will to be bound by the assurance he had given—even though the power to keep his word was not in his hands—was most certainly absolved of his duty and would have been even if he had survived Count Horn. But the King of England, in failing to keep his word by wilful intent, can no more be excused because he deferred the enactment of his treachery until after his death than the mason of whom Herodotus speaks who, having faithfully throughout his life kept the secret of the treasure house of his master, the King of Egypt, revealed all to his children as he lay dying.

In my time, I have known several cases of men who, being quite aware of their guilt in purloining the property of others, have been minded to salve their conscience by making amends in their wills to atone after their deaths. Yet in doing this, they do nothing of practical consequence: they neither set a time by which they should conclude so pressing a matter nor do they seek to right the wrong in a way that would harm them or their interests. Since they owe, they must pay—and feel the payment hurt their pocket. For the more they pay and the more it hurts, the more just and meritorious is the act of restitution. Penitence needs a burden to be carried.

Others sink lower still: those who delay, keeping for their last will and testament some hateful piece of knavery directed against someone of their acquaintance which they have kept concealed during their lifetime. And so they give the offended party cause to remember them without fondness and they also show how little they care about their conscience. For though they might fear death, they have not been able to make their malice die with them and instead extend its life beyond theirs. They are iniquitous judges, for they delay forming a judgement until they are no longer in a position to examine the facts of the case.

If I am able, I will take every care that my death shall say nothing that has not already been said by my life.

3

On Idling

Just as we see that land that is rich and fertile but fallow abounds with countless varieties of wild, unusable plants and, to make it serve a proper purpose, must be schooled and set to work by the sowing of seeds that answer to our requirements; and likewise, as we see that while unattended women may sometimes produce unformed fragments of flesh [an idea found in Plutarch's *Matrimonial Precepts*], they must work with seed other than their own in order to obtain sound and natural propagation—so it is with our minds. If they are not directed to and occupied by a specific subject which concentrates and leads them on, they will go their own sweet way, skipping hither and thither in the capricious meadows of our imagination,

as in water in a bowl of bronze the shivering reflections of the light of sun or shining moon send dapples all around and then dart up and strike the coffered ceilings above.

—Virgil, *Æneid*, VIII, 22

In that agitated state, there is no wild folly, no flight of fancy that they will not entertain,

conjuring vain phantasms, as in sick men's dreams.

—Horace, *Ars Poetica*, 7

The mind that has no firm anchor point is lost for, as is commonly said, it is nowhere if it is everywhere:

He who lives everywhere, lives nowhere.

—Martial, *Epigrams*, VII 73

When I lately retired to my manor and estate, I was resolved to do nothing except spend what remains to me of life at rest, far from the madding crowd. I felt I could not do my mind a greater service than to allow it to idle and let it look after itself, to slow down, stop and settle into its own rhythms. This, I hoped, it would do more easily now that it had become over the years more sedate and more mature. But I find that 'idleness invariably supplies unreliable thoughts' (Lucan, *Pharsalia*, IV, 704) and that on the contrary it gives itself, like a horse that bolts, far more trouble than its thrown rider would have put it to. It starts in me so many half-formed fancies and monstrous fantasies one after the other, in no order and with no thread to them, that when I stepped back to consider how odd and strange they are, I began to make a record of them, hoping thereby, in time, to make my mind blush with the shame of it.

4

On Liars

There is not a man alive less well equipped to speak of memory than I, for I scarce have any at all and firmly believe that there is not another in the whole world that is more distorting and defective than my own. The other usual faculties I have in middling, ordinary measures. But as far as Memory goes, I do believe I must be unusual, rare even, and worthy to be known—famous, even—for it.

In addition to the natural embarrassment it causes me (given how important memory is to us, Plato was surely right to call it a great and powerful goddess), it is a fact that when in my country they say that a man has no memory, what they really mean is that he is a cretin. When I complain of my poor memory, they lecture me and refuse to believe me, as they would if I were trying to make out that I was stupid. They fail to see the difference between memory and understanding, and that makes things harder for me.

But they do me wrong, for experience shows on the

contrary that an excellent memory is frequently associated with poor judgement. They further wrong me in this: I do nothing so well as friendship and the words they use to admit my infirmity make me out to be ungrateful. They question my affections by attacking my memory and turn a natural defect into a deliberate fault. They say: 'He forgot this request or that promise' or 'He does not remember his friends', or 'He has completely forgotten to do or say or not say such or such a thing as I, as a friend, had particularly asked of him.' Of course, I admit to being forgetful, but neglecting to carry out a thing my friend has asked of me, that is something I never do. They should tolerate my wretched affliction and not turn it into a form of malice of a kind that is entirely at odds with my natural temper.

Yet I do take some comfort from my forgetfulness. Firstly, because it is a flaw which provided the main reason that allowed me to correct a greater evil that might well have overtaken me, namely ambition: a poor memory does not serve anyone well who has to do with public affairs. Secondly, as is shown by various comparable examples in nature's compensatory manner of proceeding, she has strengthened other faculties of mine to make up for my dismal memory. Yet had I had the benefit of memory, I should have walked in the steps of others as most people do and, like them, picked up new ideas and novel opinions as and when they came my way. But I should not then have trained up my own mind and judgement. And thirdly, by this means, my speech is more direct and uncluttered, for the storehouse of memory is inevitably better stocked than the powerhouse of invention. Had my memory been good, I would have deafened all my friends with my chatter, the topics themselves as they arose encouraging whatever innate ability I possess to handle and expatiate on them, thus making me wax warm and at ever greater length. This would have been a pity, as I know only too well by observing the way some of my closest friends speak. Memory serves them up with their subject full and entire, but they nevertheless start their tale so far back and lard it with such irrelevances that if what they say is good, they stifle what is good in it; and if it is not good, you are left cursing the excellence of their memory or the weakness of their judgement. It is a very ticklish business either to try to interrupt or stop people talking once they are launched: there is no moment when the power of a horse is more clearly felt than when you are bringing it up short, to a dead stop. I see even those who stick to their theme unwilling and sometimes incapable of halting in their headlong discourse. Even as they cast around for a suitable point at which they might conclude, they carry on wittering and dragging matters out like men who are ready to drop from exhaustion. It is the old who are most dangerous in this respect for time long past remains fresh in their minds and they forget how often they repeat themselves. I have known tales which were once very entertaining which became utterly boring in the mouth of a great lord, each of his listeners having heard them all a hundred times before.

Secondly, I am also, as one ancient author once said, less likely to remember times when I have been wronged.

I need a list of them to remind me, like Darius who, so that he would not forget a certain offence done him by the Athenians, kept a page who every time he sat down at table would come and repeat three times in his ear: 'Sire, remember the Athenians!'.

Another thing: the places I see again and books I reread smile on me by seeming fresh and new.

There is every reason why people who do not feel sufficiently confident of their memory should not become liars. I realize that the grammarians make a distinction between 'an untruth' and 'a lie', arguing that an untruth means saying something that is false but which we believe to be true; while the definition of a lie in Latin, from which our French language is derived, designated a statement that we know in our hearts to be untrue, and that therefore it is perpetrated only by those who deliberately say something that is contrary to what they know to be true. It is of this second category I will now speak.

Now this sort of people either invent and make things up or they disguise and embroider the facts. What they change and disguise, they often alter again as they re-tell their story. But it is hard for them to avoid departing from what they said at the outset because the original facts, being the first to register in their memory, are indelibly imprinted on it, both by their grasp of them and the workings of their mind. So it is difficult for the truth not to crop up in their imagination, in which false versions put down roots which are implanted neither securely nor solidly enough and are easily dislodged, with the result that the facts of the original case continue to be permanently present in their minds and blot out memories of their later false and distorted accretions.

They have a great deal less to fear from tripping themselves up when what they say is a complete fabrication, since there is no true version that can be used to challenge and expose their mendacity. Even so, given that their invention is tenuous and difficult to fix in the mind, it may all too readily elude the control of a memory which is not entirely reliable. I have seen and been amused by many examples of this, often at the expense of men who claim that they tailor their words to fit whatever business they have in hand and to be agreeable to the great personages they are talking to. The plain fact is that cases are regularly altered by circumstances (to which they are prepared to sacrifice their honesty and good faith) and consequently their language must change accordingly, with the result that what moments before they said was grey suddenly becomes yellow; one man is told this and another that; and if by some chance those men should walk away, confer and compare their conflicting dealings, what does their fine art of negotiation amount to? Moreover, they are very careless and frequently give themselves away, for what a stupendous memory they would need to be able to remember so many variations which they have composed on the same theme! In my lifetime, I have seen many who had the ambition of acquiring this much-prized, lofty skill, but they failed to see that, though it may be highly regarded, the very fact of having a reputation for it renders it ineffective.

Lying is truly an accursed vice. We are men and have only our word to bind us together. If we fully understood the barbarity and gravity of lying, we should rightly see that it is more deserving of the stake than any other crime. I find that in the ordinary way of things people waste much time misguidedly punishing children for innocent peccadilloes and disciplining them harshly for naughty deeds which are relatively harmless and leave no trace. Lying, and one rung below it, obstinacy, seem to me to be the faults whose beginnings and development stand in greatest need of correction, for they grow as the child grows. And once the tongue has been started on this false tack, it is impossibly hard to set it to rights again. It is why we see otherwise honest men turn out to be enslaved by it. I have a tailor who is a good and decent man, yet I never once heard him say anything that was true, no, not even when it was in his interest to do so.

If, like truth, falsehood had only one face, we might be on better terms with it, because then we could simply take as true the opposite of what a liar says. But the inverse of truth has a thousand faces and an unlimited field of operations.

The Pythagoreans reckon what is good to be certain and finite and what is evil infinite and uncertain. Arrows follow a thousand paths that miss the mark: only one trajectory will lead to the bull's eye. Certainly, I could not swear in all conscience that I could ever bring myself, not even to avoid some imminent, extreme danger, to tell a brazen, bare-faced lie.

An early Church Father once said that a dog we know makes a better companion than a man whose language we do not understand—

just as one stranger to another stranger is not a man

—PLINY, *HISTORIA NATURALIS*, VII, I

—so how much less congenial is a lying tongue than silence?

King François I of France used to boast of having got completely the better of Francisque Taverna, ambassador of Francesco Sforza. This Taverna, a man famous for his golden tongue, had been sent to lift all blame from his master and justify his behaviour to His Majesty in regard to a matter of great consequence, which was this. With an eye to maintaining some channels of secret intelligence in Italy from which he had lately been driven, and particularly with the Duchy of Milan, the king had sought to insinuate a representative of his to be near the duke, in effect an ambassador but in appearance a private gentleman, who gave out that he was there on his own personal business. For the duke was much more dependent on the emperor, particularly at that time when he was negotiating the marriage of his niece, daughter of the King of Denmark (who is presently dowager duchess of Lorraine) and could not have it known that he had any contact or dealings with us without attracting much unwanted attention.

A suitable person to undertake this mission was found in a gentleman of Milan, an equerry of the king's horse, named Merveille. This man was dispatched with secret accreditation papers and instructions as an ambassador. In addition, as a cover and a pose, he also carried other letters of recommendation to the duke concerning his own private business. But he remained longer at the duke's side than was justified by such business, which made the emperor suspicious and here was, we imagine, the cause of what then ensued. What happened was that, on the pretext of a murder charge that was brought against our envoy, the duke cut off his head one fine night after a trial that lasted but two days.

The aforementioned Francisque arrived at the French court armed with a long, entirely specious account of the incident—for the king had appealed to all the Princes of Christendom and to the duke himself for an explanation—and was given a morning audience. He laid out the broad lines of his argument, then proceeded to expatiate on a number of highly plausible aspects of the case, saying that his master had never thought of this Merveille as anything other than a private gentleman and one of his subjects who was in Milan on business of his own; that the man had never lived there as anything else, even denying that he had ever heard the rumours that he was a member of the king's household, or that his Majesty knew him at all let alone well enough to appoint him as his ambassador.

Then it was the king's turn. He pressed the ambassador hard, raising a number of objections and asking various questions, hounding him on all sides until finally pinning him down by asking him about the execution which had taken place at night and, seemingly, away from prying eyes.

To which the poor man, cornered at last and hoping to put an honest face on matters, replied that the duke would not have wanted, out of respect for His Majesty who would have been upset, to hold the execution in the full light of day! It is not difficult to imagine how he struggled to hold his head up again after coming such a cropper under the very large nose of King François.

Pope Julius II dispatched an ambassador to the King of England, to stir him up against that same King François. The ambassador explained his mission during a royal audience. In replying, the King of England dwelt on the difficulties he foresaw in making the preparations that would be necessary for making war on such a powerful monarch. He gave several reasons for his hesitation. The ambassador replied most inappropriately that he had thought of them and had already drawn them to the attention of the Pope.

Now this statement was so far removed from his mission, which was to urge the King of England to take up arms and go to war at once, that it gave His Majesty the first inkling of an idea, which subsequently turned out to be true: that the ambassador in his private sympathies was on the side of France. When the Pope received a report of his envoy's conduct, he confiscated his property and the man was so disgraced that he was lucky to escape with his head still on his shoulders.

5

That We Should Not Be Considered Happy Until We Are Dead

Always wait for a man's last hour to come: no one may be said to have been happy before he is dead and buried.

—OVID, METAMORPHOSES, III, 135

On this subject, there is a story which children know, about King Crœsus who was taken captive by Cyrus and sentenced to death. As he was about to be executed, he cried out: 'Solon! Solon!' This was conveyed to Cyrus who asked him what he meant by it. Crœsus replied that he was merely proving, in his person and to his cost, the truth of the warning which Solon had once given him, namely that men, however kindly fortune might have looked on them, cannot be deemed happy until they have been seen to reach the end of the last day of their lives. For, given the uncertainty and mutability of human affairs, the smallest thing may quietly pass from one state of things to another which is very different. And yet Agesilaus, on being told by someone that the King of Persia was a happy man because he had been very young when he was raised to his present high estate, said: 'Yes, but at his age Priam was not unhappy either.' In short order, kings of Macedonia, descendants of Alexander the Great, became carpenters and scriveners in Rome and Sicilian tyrants pettifogging pedagogues in Corinth. One man who had conquered half the world and commanded many armies ended up a wretched toady among the knavish court officials of a King of Egypt: that was the price paid by great Pompey for an extra five or six months of life. And in our fathers' day, Ludovico Sforza, tenth Duke of Milan, under whom all Italy was driven and shaken for many years, was seen to die at Loches—but only after being held there ten years a prisoner, which was not the best part of his dealings with Fortune. And has not that fairest of Queens, Mary of the Scots, widow of the most powerful king in all Christendom, lately met her end by the hand of an executioner?

There are many such examples, for it might well seem that, as it is with the storms and tempests which rage against the presumption of our tall buildings, so there are spirits on high that are envious of any greatness here below.

It would seem that some unseen power bears down on the affairs of men and for its sport topples the glittering symbols and cruel weapons of power.

—LUCRETIUS, *DE RERUM NATURA*, V 1231

Fortune also appears sometimes to wait in timely ambush for the very last day of our lives before showing her power, in just one single moment, to knock down what she has taken many years to build up, so that we exclaim, with Liberius:

> *I have lived this one day longer than I should have lived.*
>
> —MACROBIUS, *SATURNALIA*, II, 7

So there is good reason to take Solon's sound advice seriously. Yet he was a philosopher, and to philosophers the favour and malice of Fortune count for nothing and rank neither as joy nor misery. For them great honours and powers are by their nature indifferent. I think it more than likely that he had some other point to make, which was to show that the happiness of life—which depends on the tranquillity and peace of a well-born mind and the resolve and confidence of a well-ordered soul—can never be assumed in a man until the curtain is first seen to fall on the final and doubtless most toilsome act of his life's drama. There may be disguise and dissembling in all the rest of his days, when the fine arguments of philosophy play only minor parts and dramatic turns do not test us to the quick but allow us time to maintain unperturbed our settled outlook. But in the contest between ourselves and death, there can be no more pretending: we must speak frankly and reveal what is good and clear at the bottom of the pot:

> *Only then are honest words spoken from the heart; the mask is off and only truth remains.*
>
> —LUCRETIUS, *DE RERUM NATURA*, III, 57

Which is why at this extreme moment all the other actions of our life are to be tried and tested. It is the culminating day, the day that gives its ruling on all the days that have gone before, the day, as one ancient author said, which passes judgement on all of my preceding years. I shall delegate to my death the task of delivering the verdict on the fruit of all my studies. We shall see then if my writings came from my tongue or from my heart.

I know of many who by dying have put the mark of good or bad on their living. Scipio, Pompey's father-in-law, rehabilitated when he died a good death the poor opinion that had been held of him up to that moment. When Epaminondas was asked which of these three he regarded the most highly, Chabrias, Iphicrates or himself, he replied: 'A man would need to see them die before he could give a proper answer to that.' Indeed, it would take much away from Epaminondas were he to be judged without regard to the honour and distinction of his death.

God made all things as it pleased him best. And yet in my lifetime three of the most execrable men that I have ever known, who exemplified the life abominable and even incarnated infamy itself, died orderly deaths, remaining serene in all respects and perfectly composed.

There are brave deaths and charmed deaths. I have seen the Reaper snap the thread of one career made of prodigious leaps forward and, in the full flowering of its enlargement, inflict on a certain person [Montaigne's friend Étienne de la Boétie] so glorious a death that, in my view, his bold and generous ambitions were never so sublime as their sudden curtailment. For he reached his goal without arriving at his intended destination and did so with more honour and glory than he could have hoped or wished for. In this wise did he, by his dying, find a quicker route to the fame and influence to which his chosen career aspired.

In the judgement I make of the lives of others, I always take particular note of the manner of their ending. Among the principal concerns that I have for my own is the hope that I will die well, which is to say patiently and without fuss.

PART TWO

On the Pursuit of Reason

As his device, Montaigne chose Que sais-je? By it, he meant not 'what do I know?' but 'what do I know that I know to be true?' A central concern was therefore to learn, by observing the processes of thinking—his own, that of others and, not least, of ancient authors—how to prepare the mind to reach rational conclusions. His goal was to acquire a mental discipline that excluded superstition, unquestioned tradition, supposition, hearsay and unreliable evidence and adhered strictly to what is objective, provable and logical. His scepticism informed his Humanist (human-centred) approach to thinking. As a result, to the clear sense the reader acquires of Montaigne's surprisingly modern outlook is added the impression of a mind of striking clarity.

6

On Fear

I was paralysed by fear, my hair stood on end and my voice stuck in my throat.

—Virgil, *Æneid*, II, 774

I am not what they call a 'natural scientist' and know next to nothing of the manner and means by which fear acts on and in us. But it is a strange passion and the doctors say that there is no other which so quickly drives out our judgement from its established place. I have seen many men paralysed by fear and it is obvious that while the fit lasts it can produce the most terrible irrationality in even the most level-headed of them. I am not talking about the common people in whom it creates images of ancestors risen from their graves, still wrapped in their shrouds, or of half-human monsters, werewolves and goblins. But even among soldiers, where it should have a lesser hold, how often has it transformed a flock of sheep into a squadron of knights in armour, reeds and bulrushes into men-at-arms and lancers, friends into foes, and the white cross of France into the red standard of Spain?

When Monsieur de Bourbon captured Rome, an ensign posted as a guard at Borgo San Pietro was so overcome by fright at the sound of the first alarm, that he flung himself banner in hand through a breach in the city wall and bore down on the enemy, thinking he was heading back into the town. Eventually, when he saw the troops of Monsieur de Bourbon forming into lines to face his charge (for they believed that here was a sortie mounted by the city's defenders), he realized his mistake and, turning tail, fled back through the same breach from which he had emerged before running across three hundred yards of open terrain.

No lot as happy as that standard-bearer's lucky escape fell to Captain Juille's ensign who, when Saint-Paul was taken from us by the Comte de Bures and Monsieur du Reu, was so overcome by fear that he hurled himself, standard and all, through a loophole and was cut to pieces by the enemy. And at the same siege, it was a memorable attack of fear that so clutched, shrank and froze the heart of a gentleman that he dropped down quite dead in a breach without any visible kind of wound.

A similar fear has sometimes gripped whole multitudes. In one of the battles of Germanicus against the Alemanni, two large bodies of troops took such fright that one rode straight to the place from which their enemies had just fled.

Sometimes, as in the case of the first two examples, fear lends wings to our heels. At others, it nails our feet to the ground and attaches a ball and chain to our ankles, as in the account of how the Emperor Theophilus, in the battle he lost against the Agorenes, was so crippled and crushed by fear that he did not even have the wits to run away—'so deep does fear run that it fears even help' (Quintus Curtius, *Historiæ Alexandri Magni*, III, ii)—until Manuel, one of the principal captains of his army, seized him roughly, shook him, as if waking him from a deep sleep, and said: 'Sire, if you do not follow me, I will kill you, for it would be better that you die now than be taken prisoner and lose your empire.'

But fear reserves its worst for times when, in its grip, we are thrown back on our valour which it has first weakened by robbing us of all sense of duty and honour. In the first pitched battle which the Romans lost against Hannibal, when Sempronius was Consul, a force of over ten thousand foot soldiers was unmanned by dread. But, failing to find a safe route and passage by which to make their cowardly escape, they launched themselves at the great mass of their enemies and, with a superhuman effort, broke through their ranks with a great slaughter of Carthaginians, thus achieving igno-minious flight for the same price as would have bought them a glorious victory.

The thing I fear most is fear. It is more cruel by far than any other adversity that befalls us. What other emotion is there that could be both more afflicting and more fitting than that of Pompey's friends who were on board his ship when they saw the horrid massacre of his navy? But fear at the sight of the Egyptian vessels which had begun to bear down on them so exceeded their horror that they were seen to take no action save to urge their sailors to make haste away and the oarsmen to pull hard until they arrived at Tyre where, free now of fear, they had leisure to turn their thoughts to what they had done and give way to lamentations and tears which had been suspended by the greater power of their fear.

Then fear drives out all wisdom from my mind.

—ENNIUS, AP. CICERO, *TUSCULANÆ DISPUTATIONES*, IV, 8.

Men who have been engaged in some skirmish of war, with wounds still running with blood, may sometimes be returned to the field. But men who have developed an utter terror of the enemy you will never persuade to stand firm and look him in the eye again. People who have a deep fear of losing their possessions, of facing banishment or enslavement, live in a state of continuous apprehension, unable to drink or eat or sleep, whereas the genuinely poor, those who are already exiles and slaves, often live as happily as anyone else. And many who, when pierced by the arrows of fear, have hung or drowned themselves or leapt from high places, teach us only too well that fear is even more insistent and unbearable than death itself.

The Greeks recognized another kind of fear quite different from what we have spoken of thus far, saying that it has no apparent cause but is an emanation from heaven. Whole nations may be struck down by it, even entire armies. It was one such visitation that brought Carthage to stupendous desolation. The only sounds to be heard were screams and terrified voices. The inhabitants were seen to run out of their houses, as if a general alarum had been sounded. They began attacking, wounding and killing each other as though they were enemies who had come to occupy their city. All was chaos and turmoil until at last, by dint of orisons and sacrifices, they had appeased the wrath of their gods.

This the Greeks called Panic Terror.

7

To Tell True from False,
It Is Folly to Rely on Our Own Capacities

There is a reason why we attribute to simple-mindedness or ignorance both the ease with which we believe things and our readiness to let ourselves be convinced. I seem to recall once having been told that belief was a kind of impression engraved on our mind. And the more receptive and unresisting the mind, the easier it is to write indelibly on it.

> As the scale of a balance descends when weights are put on it,
> so the mind yields to clear explanation.

—CICERO, *ACADEMICA*, II, 12

Thus when the mind is empty and with no ballast to counter it, it gives way more easily to the weight of the first argument that is put unto it. This is why children, the common people, women and the sick are more amenable to being led by the nose.

But, on the other hand, it is equally foolish and presumptuous to excoriate and dismiss as untrue anything that seems implausible to us. This is a common error committed by those who believe they have some competence above the average. I myself used to be guilty of this mistake. Once, if I ever heard talk of the walking dead, divinations, spells, witchcraft or matters of some other like sort that I could not swallow—

> *dreams, magic terrors, miracles, witches, ghosts in the night or portents from Thessalonia*

—HORACE, *EPISTOLÆ*, II, III, 208

—I would feel sorry for the hapless people who were taken in by such nonsense. But now I see that I was at least as much to be pitied as they. Not that experience has helped me to see further than my early beliefs (though not from any lack of curiosity on my part) but reason has taught me that rejecting something out of hand as untrue and utterly false is to claim to know the limits and limitations both of the will of God and of the power of Nature, our Mother. I also learnt that there is no folly in the world greater than to reduce both powers to our level and our capacities. If we call everything beyond the reach of our reason monstrous or miraculous, how many more such manifestations will go on surfacing? Consider through what fogs and mists we have groped our way to a proper knowledge of what we already hold secure in our hands and we shall find that it is familiarity with things rather than study of them that removes their strangeness.

*Few now, if any, look up at the radiant temple of the heavens,
being so used to the sight.*

—LUCRETIUS, *DE RERUM NATURA*, II, 1037–8

For if such things were offered to us to see for the very first
time, we would think they were just as—or even more—unbe-
lievable than any others.

*Imagine that they [the sun and moon] were suddenly revealed
to mortals: what greater wonders could there be than these
which, before they saw them, the peoples of the world would
not have dared believe?*

—LUCRETIUS, *DE RERUM NATURA*, II, 1032–5

The man who had never before seen a river believed the first
one he came to must be the sea. And those things that to the
best of our knowledge we believe to be the biggest we have
seen, we think must be the absolute largest that nature can
make of that kind.

*A river may appear huge to a man who never saw one that was
bigger; and in the same way, the biggest man or tree will seem
huge, and we will believe them to be the hugest of their sort.*

—LUCRETIUS, *DE RERUM NATURA*, VI, 674

*Things grow familiar to our minds by dint of being often seen;
and so we cease to be amazed by them, nor are we curious to
know how they came about.*

—CICERO, *DE NATURA DEORUM*, II, 38

It is the novelty of things, not their size, that prompts us to enquire into their cause.

We should judge the infinite power of nature with greater reverence and be more prepared to acknowledge our ignorance and deficiencies. How many highly implausible things have been told us by highly reputable people? We might not be convinced, but we must suspend our doubts because to dismiss such things out of hand as being impossible is to set ourselves up with crass presumption as judges who know the limits of the possible. If we understood the difference between the possible and the merely unexpected or what runs counter both to the natural order of things and to the general opinion of mankind, we should be neither rashly credulous nor glibly sceptical, and thus follow the policy of 'Nothing to excess' recommend by Chilo.

When we are told by Froissart that the Comte de Foix, then in the Béarn, received news of the defeat of King John of Castille at Aljubarotta on the day after it happened, and read of the manner in which he came by the news, we may well smile. And we may also laugh when we read in the annals that on the very day that King Phillip-Augustus died at Mantua, Pope Honorious publicly solemnized his funeral and decreed that all Italy should do likewise. For it is doubtful that the authority of these witnesses has sufficient credibility to detain us.

But that is not all. When Plutarch, in addition to various examples he finds in antiquity, claims to know with unimpeachable certainty that, in the time of Domitian, news of the battle lost by Antony in distant Germany several days before was published in Rome—and was spread throughout the whole world—on the very day that it was fought; and when Cæsar says that news of a happening often preceded the event itself, might we not say, to explain why those guileless people allowed themselves to be taken in by vulgar report, that they were not as clear-sighted as we are? Yet is there anything subtler, more transparent and sharper than Pliny's judgement when he decides to use it, and nothing that less resembles trivial musing? I leave to one side the excellence or otherwise of his knowledge by which I am much less impressed. But in which of those two attributes are we superior to him? And yet, the merest schoolboy could catch him out in a lie and also teach him a thing or two about the works of nature.

When we read Bouchet's account of the miracles performed through the relics of Saint Hilary, we can let it go: his authority is not so great as to deny us the freedom to challenge him. But to go from there to summarily dismissing all accounts of that kind would seem to me singularly unwise. The great Saint Augustine himself bears witness of having seen, in Milan, how a child's sight was restored by the relics of Saints Gervasius and Protasius; how a woman of Carthage was cured of a cancer by the sign of the cross made over her by a recently baptized woman; how Hesperius, one of his circle, using a little of the earth from the sepulchre of Our Lord, banished evil spirits which haunted his house and how, when this same earth was transported to the church, a paralytic was instantly healed by it; how a woman in a procession touched the reliquary of Saint Stephen with a posy of flowers, then rubbed her eyes with the posy and recovered her long-lost sight; and how he had himself been present when other miracles had occurred. What charges shall we bring against him and two holy bishops—Aurelius and Maximinimus—on whom he calls to attest the truth of these things? Ignorance or simple-mindedness or naivety or malice or fraud? Is there any man in our times with nerve enough to claim that he compares with them in either virtue or piety or knowledge, judgement or competency?

> *Who, if they give no reasons, thinks they can convince me by relying on their authority alone?*

—CICERO, *TUSCULANÆ DISPUTATIONES*, I. 21

To look down on things which we do not understand is bold and dangerous, a matter of great consequence, to say nothing of the absurd presumption that comes with it. For, when you have trusted to your infallible understanding to establish the difference between what is true and what is false and find that you are forced to believe things even stranger than those you have already dismissed, you have no choice but to abandon your fine distinctions. What I feel creates such turmoil in our consciences, in the current religious crisis, is that Catholics make too light of their faith. They think they are being moderate and tolerant when they surrender to their [Protestant] opponents certain of the articles under discussion. But beyond that, they fail to see the advantage they hand to the opposition when they give ground and retreat, and how it encourages the enemy to press its case the harder by concentrating on those articles which they deem least important but may in fact often be central and crucial. Either we must get solidly behind the authority of our ecclesiastical polity or abandon it altogether. It is not for us to choose which parts of it to obey.

But that is not all. I can say this because I have tried it myself, having in the past used my personal freedom to pick and choose which articles of our Church observance to follow or reject because they seemed to me either pointless or puzzling. But when I later came to discuss them with learned men, I found those same things in fact to be set foursquare on a very solid basis and that it is stupidity and ignorance which lead us to treat those articles with less reverence than the others.

Why does it not occur to us to be aware of the contradictions in our own judgements? How many things which yesterday were unquestioned beliefs do we think of today as fairy tales? Curiosity and the quest for fame are the twin banes of our waking lives. The former drives us to poke our noses into everything, and the latter refuses to let us leave any stone unturned and any question unanswered.

8

On How We Can Cry and Laugh
at the Same Thing

When we read in the history books that Antigonus was not at all grateful to his son for presenting him with the head of his enemy, King Pyrrhus, who had just been killed while fighting against him, and that on seeing it he burst into tears; also that René, Duke of Lorraine, lamented the demise of Duke Charles of Burgundy, whom he had recently defeated, and at his funeral wore full mourning; or again that when, after the battle of Auroy which the Count de Montfort won against Charles of Blois, his rival for the Duchy of Brittany, the victor came across the body of his slain foe, he was visibly overcome by grief—when we read of such things, we should not just exclaim:

Thus it happens that the mind hides every emotion under a cloak of its opposite, so that now all seems light, now dark.

—PLUTARCH, *LIFE OF PYRRHUS*, XVI

When Cæsar was presented with the head of Pompey, the histories say that he turned his eyes away as if from an ugly and unpleasant object. There had long been between them such a common bond and understanding in the management of public affairs, in the commonality of their wealth, in the many mutual services rendered and joint actions taken, that we should not believe that the look on his face was forced or false, as another historian claims:

> *Thinking it safe now to play the affectionate father-in-law, he wept tears that were not spontaneous and uttered groans that rose from a joyous heart.*

> —LUCAN, *PHARSALIA*, IX, 1037

For though it is true that most of our actions are all façade and veneer and that it may sometimes be true that

> *the tears of an heir are but smiles behind a mask.*

> —AULUS GELLIUS, IN PUBLILIUS SYRUS, *SENTENTIA* XVII, 14

Yet when we come to judge these things, we must recognize that our souls are often agitated by a variety of conflicting passions. Furthermore, it is said that there are assembled in our bodies sundry humours among which one is dominant and ordinarily commands us according to our natural temper; also that in our soul, though it may be unsettled by the various motions which ruffle it, there must of necessity be one main contender that stands out above the rest. But, given the clamouring and changeability of the soul, no such domination is needed by those lesser motions to rise in their turn to occupy the commanding height and lead a modest charge. Which is why we see not only children innocently follow nature and laugh and cry at the same thing, but must admit also that none of us can set out on a journey gladly undertaken for his own pleasure without feeling his heart sink at the prospect of saying farewell to family and friends; and if he does not shed actual tears at least he puts his foot in the stirrup with a face that is glum and overcast. And however bright the fond flame that warms the hearts of well-born young brides, they still must be torn by force from the embrace of their mothers who fetch them to their husbands, no matter what this good fellow says:

> *Is Venus really so repellent to new brides?*
> *Or do they respond to the joy of parents with false tears*
> *And shed them copiously, even as they enter the nuptial chamber?*
> *No, by the gods, their weeping is a fraud.*

> —CATULLUS, *COMA BERENICES*, LXVI, 15

This is why it is not strange to lament the passing of a man who we would not wish to see still living.

When I get angry with my valet, I do not choose my words, my curses are sincere not feigned. But once the fit has passed and if he needs my help for anything, I will gladly do whatever I can for him and instantly turn the page. When I call him knave or coxcomb it is never my intention to pin these names on him permanently, nor do I believe that I am contradicting myself if moments later I call him an honest man. No single attribute can sum us up entire. If talking to oneself were not the badge of a madman, there would scarce be a day when I would not be heard grumbling to myself about myself: 'You fool!' But no, I would not want that word to be the one that defines me.

Anyone who sees me act cold or, conversely, loving towards my wife and concludes that the one or the other of these sentiments is a pretence is an ass. As Nero took his leave of his mother even as he sent her away to be drowned, yet he nevertheless felt the full impact of this final maternal farewell and was filled with horror and pity.

They say the light of the Sun is not all one continuous stream but made up of separate rays constantly beamed down at us one after the other and so thickly that we cannot make out the gaps between them.

For with the overflowing spring of liquid light the ethereal sun floods the heavens, and with an even flow of dazzling fresh radiance speedily supplies new light in lieu of old.

—LUCRETIUS, *DE RERUM NATURA*, V, 282

So in like manner does our mind scatter its whims and itches, in ways that are diverse and barely perceptible.

Artabanus once took his nephew Xerxes by surprise and chided him for the sudden change of expression on his face. At that time he was thinking about the colossal size of his forces crossing the Hellespont in his campaign against Greece. First he experienced a shiver of pleasure at the sight of the thousands of men under his command and let it show in the jubilation and liveliness of his countenance. Then suddenly, in a single instant, the thought came into his mind that each one of this great number of lives would have ended within, at most, a century, and he knitted his brows and grew sad enough for tears.

We have all resolutely undertaken to avenge an injury and experienced that singular feeling of satisfaction which victory brings—and yet we weep for it too. But it is not for the facts of the case that we cry: nothing has changed there. However, our mind now contemplates them in a different light and puts a fresh complexion on them. For every thing under the sun can have several faces and divers facets. Family relations, old acquaintances and long-standing friendships can grip our imagination and for a time possess it according to who and what they are. But their exits and their entrances happen so quickly that they escape us.

> *Nothing moves so swiftly than the mind when it is set on the thing to be done. Once roused to act it is speedier than any thing to be seen in nature.*
>
> —LUCRETIUS, *DE RERUM NATURA*, III, 183

Which is why we deceive ourselves if we try to gather this swift succession of partial sightings into one seamless whole. When Timoleon weeps for the murder he has committed after so much mature and noble deliberation, he is not weeping for the freedom which has been restored to his homeland, he does not weep for the Tyrant: it is for his brother that he weeps. One part of his duty is performed; let us leave him to perform the other.

9

On Solitude

Let us set to one side the never-ending comparisons between the solitary and the active life and likewise the fine words which greed and ambition use to cover the nakedness of their self-interest by insisting that we are not born for our solitary selves but for the broader public. Instead let us boldly refer the question to those who dance to that tune and invite them to examine their consciences and tell us whether titles, public office and the harassing hurly-burly of the world are not, on the contrary, sought after simply as a way of making private profit at the expense of society at large. The squalid means used in our century to climb the ladder of success show clearly that its objective is equally squalid and shabby. Let us answer Ambition and say that it is she who gives us our taste for solitude, for what does she avoid more than the company of others? What does she seek more than private room for manoeuvre? Of course, there are opportunities galore to do good or evil anywhere, yet if the contention of Bias of Priene be true, namely that there is more in the world of the first than of the second, plus what is said in *Ecclesiastes* (7, v.28) that 'One [good] man in a thousand have I not found'—

> *To be sure, good men are rare; they number barely more*
> *than there are gates to Thebes or mouths to the rich Nile*

—JUVENAL, *SATIRÆ*, XIII, 26

—then the danger of being contaminated is clearly greatest in a crowd. There is a choice: either become like those who are unprincipled, or hate them. It is equally dangerous to become like them, because they are many, and to hate many of them, because they are not like us.

Merchants who put to sea are right to insist that those who travel in the same vessel with them be not dissolute, blasphemous and wicked, for they judge such company to bode ill. That is why Bias jokingly said to passengers and crew who were facing the danger of a great tempest with him and were calling on the gods for help: 'Keep silent, otherwise *they* will know that you are here with me!'

And, in a more telling instance, Albuquerque, Viceroy in India of Emmanuel, King of Portugal, in a moment of extreme peril at sea, set a young boy on his shoulders for the sole reason that by joining their fates together the boy's innocence might be a safeguard and a recommendation to divine favour to bring him safe home to port again.

It is not the case that a wise man cannot live content anywhere, nor be alone among the denizens of a palace. But if free to choose, he will tell you that he would rather flee and avoid the very sight of them. He will tolerate them if he must, but if left to his own devices, he will choose to go. He does not feel that he has sufficiently stripped himself of his own vices if he must continue to contend with the vices of others.

Charondas punished as being wicked those who were found guilty of keeping wicked company.

There is nothing that is both so unsociable and so sociable as human nature: the first because of our vices and the latter by our nature. Now Antisthenes does not seem to me to have given a satisfactory answer to the man who rebuked him for his dealings with evil persons by saying that doctors survive well enough in the close company of the sick. For though they attend to the health of the ill, they endanger their own in courting contagion by constantly seeing and treating disease.

Now, I take it that our goal is always the same, namely, to live at peace and at our ease. But people do not all set about seeking quietude in the right way. Often a man may think he has given up his occupation when all he has done is exchange one employment for another: there is scarce any less worry involved in managing a family than there is in managing an entire kingdom. And when a mind has troubles, it has time for nothing else: while domestic matters may be the least important of problems, they are no whit less bothersome. Moreover, although we may have escaped the grip of courts and commerce, we have not freed ourselves of the main vexations of life:

*It is reason and discretion that take away our cares, not a high
seat that overlooks a wide prospect of the sea.*

—HORACE, *EPISTOLAE*, I, XI, 25–26

Ambition, avarice, lack of resolve, fear and envy do not desert
us just because we move on to pastures new—

behind the mounted rider sits black care

—HORACE, *ODES*, III, I, 40

—they often pursue us even into cloisters and academies of
philosophy. Neither deserts nor rocky caves, not hair shirts
nor fasts can rid us of them:

The fatal arrow is embedded in her side.

—VIRGIL, *ÆNEID*, IV, 73

Socrates was told that such and such a man had returned from
his travels no better than when he went. 'I quite believe it,' he
said, 'for when he left he took himself with him.'

*Why do we seek change by moving to climes warmed by other suns?
Can the man who flees his native land ever escape from himself?*

—HORACE, *ODES*, II, XVI, 18

Unless a man first unburdens himself and his mind of the
worries that plague them both, uprooting him will only
make them weigh more heavily, as the cargo of a ship gives

less trouble when it is securely stowed. You will do a patient more harm than good by moving him from one place to another: by disturbing him, you will tamp his sickness down more compactly, as with stakes which, when worked to and fro and up and down, can be driven further in and will embed themselves more firmly. This is why it is not enough just to live apart from other people, nor simply to move away to another place: we must cleanse ourselves of the ways and moods of the herd which are within us. We must seek seclusion and revert to our natural selves.

> *You will say: 'I have thrown off my bonds!' But a dog, after a struggle, may also break his leash; yet when he runs away he drags a length of the chain behind him that still hangs round his neck.*

> —PERSIUS, *SATIRÆ*, V, 158

We too carry our chains with us, for the freedom we have is not complete. We still cast our eyes back to what we have left behind and our mind is full of it.

> *But unless the heart is purged, what battles must we fight and dangers face despite our will? What bitter cares still harass the troubled man, and what fears besides! what of pride, lust and anger and the havoc that they work? what of self-indulgence and sloth?*

> —LUCRETIUS, *DE RERUM NATURA*, V, 4

Our misery lies in the mind from which there is no escape:

it is the mind that is at fault, and the mind cannot flee from itself.

—HORACE, *EPISTOLAE*, I, XIX, 13

So we must call the mind to heel and return it to our natural temper: that is true solitude, and though it can be achieved in the bustle of cities and the courts of kings it is enjoyed most advantageously when we are far from the fray.

Since therefore we propose to live alone and dispense with the company of others, let us ensure that our contentment shall derive solely from ourselves. Let us abandon the ties that bind us close to other people. Let us aim to acquire over ourselves the self-assurance to live alone and at our ease.

Stilpo escaped the great fire that destroyed his city and in which he had lost wife, children and possessions. Demetrius Poliorcetes, seeing him in the midst of the general ruin of his native city yet with a face that was undismayed, asked him if he had not himself suffered a great loss. He answered No and said he had lost, thank God, nothing that was truly his own. This is also what the philosopher Antisthenes said, with a smile: a man should supply himself only with things of value that do not sink in water and can float away from a shipwreck with him.

It is true that a man of understanding has lost nothing if he still has himself.

When the city of Nola was razed by Barbarians, Paulinus, who was bishop of the place, though he had lost everything and was a captive, prayed thus to God: 'O Lord, keep me from feeling my loss, for thou knowest that as yet these Barbarians have taken nothing from me that is mine.' The riches that made him rich and the goods that made him good had survived intact. There you have what it means to take care to choose possessions which are immune to depredation and to keep them in a place where no one can enter and whose location is known only to oneself. He who is able may have wives, children, riches and, above all, good health; but we should not become so attached to them that our felicity depends on them. We must always have a secret place or niche of our very own, free and untrammelled, and in it keep our true freedom—our principal refuge—and our private self. This we must make the place where we commune exclusively with ourselves and keep it so particular to us that no outside companionship or concerns can enter there. There we may talk and laugh as though we had neither wife or children nor possessions or attendants or servants so that, should it chance that we no longer have them, it would not be novel to be obliged to do without them. We have a self that is unassailable and sufficient company. It is able to attack and defend, to receive and to give. We should not fear that in our solitude we shall sink beneath the weight of idleness and boredom.

When alone, be your own company.

—Tibullus, *Elegiæ*, VI, XIII, 12

'Virtue,' said Antisthenes, 'is sufficient unto itself and does not need discipline or words or deeds.'

Of our daily activities, there is not one in a thousand that has anything to do with our inner self. The man you see now clambering up the ruins of that city wall, hot with battle, incensed and the heedless target of many harquebusiers, and then this other defender, heavily scarred, faint and pale with hunger, determined to die rather than open the gates for him: do you think they are there for their own sakes? No, they are no doubt there on account of someone else, a man they never set eyes on who, being entirely given up to idleness and pleasure, does not give them a moment's thought. And that man, sniffling, bleary-eyed and unkempt, who you see emerging from his study after midnight, do you think that he has been riffling through his books looking for ways of becoming a better man, happier and wiser? No fear of that. He will teach posterity how to scan the verse of Plautus or the correct spelling of a Latin word, or die in the attempt.

Who is not only too ready to exchange health, repose and life itself for reputation and fame, the paltriest, most futile and falsest of the false coin in circulation among us? Since our own death does not strike dread enough in us, let us fear instead for the deaths of our wives, our children and our household. If our own affairs have not given us enough to worry about, then let us add to our troubles and bludgeon our brains by interfering in those of our friends and neighbours.

Ah! that a man should ready his mind for something that is dearer to him than he is to himself!

—TERENCE, *ADELPHŒ*, I, 1, 13

To me, it seems, following the example of Thales, that solitude is a more attractive and reasonable thing to those who have given their best and most productive years to society. Having lived enough for others, let us now live out the remaining span of our lives for ourselves. Let us settle our thoughts and intentions on us and our well-being. It is no light task to arrange for our withdrawal from society, for it causes enough trouble in itself without adding extraneous concerns. So since God gives us leave to manage how we withdraw, let us make our preparations for it: we will pack our bags and allow time to take our leave of our acquaintance. We will undo the powerful links that bind us to the things which come between us and ourselves. We must put an end to all strong obligations, and though a man might love this or that he should cleave to nothing and no one but himself. Which is to say: let what is left be our own, but not joined and glued so fast that its grip cannot be loosened without tearing the skin and gouging out some part of ourselves. For the most important thing of all is to be your own self.

It is time for us to wean ourselves off society, since there is nothing more that we can now contribute to it. A man with nothing to lend must not think of borrowing. Our powers fail us, so we must call them in and gather them to ourselves for our own use. Let the man who can throw off and curtail all the trappings of friendship and social living do so. But he should not allow the decay of age, which makes him useless, a burden and a nuisance to others, make him also useless, a burden and a nuisance to himself. He may pamper himself and pat himself on the back, but above all let him so rule himself, that he respects his reason, fears his conscience and will thus feel no shame if he trips up in their presence.

For it is rare that men respect themselves enough.

—QUINTILIAN, *INSTITUTIO ORATORIA*, X, 7

Socrates says that the young should get themselves educated, that mature men should devote themselves to doing good, that the old should withdraw from all civil and military service and live as they see fit without obligation to perform any particular public role.

Some dispositions are more suited to these precepts for retirement than others. Those whose grasp of things is feeble and blunted, whose affections are shallow and whose will is weak and do not easily obey orders or take to employment (among which number I count myself as much by inclination as by reflection), will follow such counsel more readily than other more active, committed souls who take an interest in everything, throw themselves into the fray, are passionately curious and will volunteer, step up to the mark and put themselves forward on all occasions. We must take advantage of any circumstances occurring arbitrarily and independently of us if they suit our purposes, but without placing too much reliance on them. Our mainstay they can never be, for neither reason nor nature would have it so. Why would we make our happiness dependent on the power and laws of others? Why anticipate what fate may bring? And why deprive ourselves of the comforts we still have to hand, as some have done through religion and others according to philosophical principles, who have no servant but themselves, sleep on the bare ground, put their own eyes out, throw all their money into a river and go out of their way to suffer pain. The first sort do it to gain eternal bliss in the next life at the expense of agony in this one, and the second to exclude the possibility of falling any further by sitting on the lowest step they can find. Both are the product of virtue taken to extremes. The sternest and most resolute of such natures will even make their sequestered retreats seem gorgeous and exemplary:

> *I commend the carefree, humble life and when funds run low I*
> *make bravely do with meagre fare. But when something better*
> *and more luxurious comes along, then, though I am the same*
> *person, I say that only those are wise and live well who convert*
> *their money into handsome villas.*

—Horace, *Epistolae*, I, xv, 42

Personally, I think I have more than enough to do with without going to such lengths. I find it enough, while fortune favours me, to ready myself for its disfavour and at my leisure picture (insofar as my imagination can conceive of such things) the forms in which misfortune might come upon me. It is much the same as what we do when in times of peace we use jousts and tournaments to prepare ourselves for war.

I do not reckon that Arcesilaus the philosopher was any the less virtuous because I know he used bowls and dishes made of gold and silver whenever the state of his purse allowed. Indeed I think the more of him for making a moderately liberal use of them than if he had got rid of them altogether.

I see very well how far the limits of our natural needs can extend. When I consider that the poor beggar man at my door is often haler and heartier than I am, I put myself in his shoes and try to see the world as he sees it. From there, proceeding by other examples, though I think I hear death, penury, ridicule and sickness snapping at my heels, I have no difficulty persuading myself not to be alarmed by what a lesser man than I tolerates with such forbearance. I do not accept that a deficient understanding can accomplish more than clarity of mind is capable of, or that thinking and reflection will direct us more readily than habit and custom. And knowing how slender is the thread by which those secondary expedients hang, I never weary, even at the height of my pleasures, of beseeching God to grant my most heartfelt wish, that he make me content with the way I am and with whatever amiable qualities are in me. I see sprightly young men who go nowhere without a case in which they keep a mass of pills to be used when colds come on them, for they fear rheums less when they believe they have the cure to hand. That is what everyone should do—but don't stop there. If you know you are vulnerable to some serious form of illness, lay up a supply of specifics which will soothe and deaden the affected part.

The occupation we choose to suit this style of life must be neither too demanding nor too pedestrian, for otherwise nothing will make us think it worth retiring in order to do it. It will depend on each man's particular humour. In my case, my humour does not run to managing my estate. But those who do like this activity should indulge it only sparingly.

> *They should strive to make things answer to them and not them to things.*
>
> —HORACE, *EPISTOLAE*, I, I, 19

Otherwise the stewardship of estates is, as Sallust calls it, a servile occupation. Even so, there is something to be said for it, for example a delight in gardening—which Xenophon attributes to Cyrus. It is also possible to find a midway point between, on the one hand, its rude, unforgiving toil, which is burdensome and full of care as may be seen even in those who devote themselves to it and, on the other, the utter, extreme unconcern which lets everything run to seed.

> *Democritus' cattle ate the crops in his fields while his mind took flight and wandered outside his body.*
>
> —HORACE, *EPISTOLAE*, I, XII, 12

But let us hear the advice which Pliny the Younger gave to his friend Cornelius Rufus on the subject of solitude:

'I recommend you, here in this broad, lush retreat where you now live, to leave to your serving-men the base and degrading care of the estate and devote yourself to the study of your books, striving to extract from them something which is entirely and exclusively your own.'

What he was really talking about was reputation. His thrust was similar to that of Cicero when he said he wanted to use his solitude and distance from public affairs to acquire through his writings a name that would live forever.

Is what you know nothing to you unless somebody else knows that you know?

—PERSIUS, *SATIRÆ*, I, 23

True, it seems reasonable enough that when a man talks of withdrawing from the world, he should look outside himself. But that sort only do it by halves. They make plans for their life of retirement in advance, in anticipation of the time when they will no longer be part of the world they intend to leave. And yet they go on claiming the advantages of that world though they are no longer part of it—it is a ludicrous contradiction.

The approach of those who are religiously inclined and go in search of solitude, filling their hearts with the guarantee of the divine promise of the life that is to come, is much more solidly based. They have their eyes on God, an object of infinite goodness and might; in Him they have endless matter on which their souls can glut their every desire in total freedom. Pain and suffering are grist to their mill, for they are the means of acquiring both healing and eternal bliss; even death may be welcome as a route to a perfect life. The severity of monastic rule is soon softened by the habit of it, and carnal appetites are quenched and lulled to sleep by being denied (for nothing keeps them awake more than habit and practice). This goal of a blessedly immortal new life fully warrants that we renounce the ease and comforts of the life that we have. And the man who can truly and constantly fire his soul with the flame of burning faith and hope shall make for himself a life that is agreeable and sweet beyond all other modes of existence.

I am not happy with either the end or the proposed means to it contained in Pliny's counsel, since scarce a day passes when we do not jump out of one frying pan into yet another frying pan. For example, burying oneself in books can be as painful as any other kind of self-occupation and no better for our health—which ought to be our principal concern. Nor should we let ourselves be addicted to the pleasures of reading, for it is the same pleasure that becomes the bane of the life of the gardener, the miser, the voluptuary and the man of ambition.

Philosophers are forever warning us to beware the insidious power of appetite and to distinguish between pleasures that are true and wholesome and those that are mixed and shot through with pain. Because, they say, most pleasures lure and enfold us in their embrace the better to suffocate us after the manner of the robbers which the Egyptians called Philistae.

But if our heads ached *before* we got drunk, we would surely take care not to drink too much. Yet our senses goad us: they walk on in front of us making sure to conceal what comes in their wake. Books are agreeable but if reading too many of them leads to a loss of good humour and well-being, which are our most vital assets, then we must give them up. I am one of those who believe that the joy of books does not compensate for such losses.

Just as men weakened by some long-standing indisposition of the body will at the last put themselves at the mercy of medicine and are prescribed certain rules by which to live that must not be transgressed, so the man who withdraws from the world, wearied and sickened by being too much with others, is obliged to remake his new life according to the rules of reason, and give it shape and order based on serious forethought and reflection. He must have cut all links with any kind of employment, whatever its nature, and generally turn away from the passions which intrude upon the quiet tranquillity of body and soul, and follow the path best suited to his nature:

let every man choose his own true way.

—PROPERTIUS, *ELEGIÆ*, II, xxv, 38

Whether attending to his estates, studying, hunting or engaged in any other activity, he must pursue pleasure to its utmost limits and refrain from venturing further into areas on which trouble and toil encroach. Labour and occupation must play a role but only insofar as they keep us sound in body and protect us from the unwanted consequences which attend upon that opposite extreme: lax and neglectful idleness.

There are kinds of learning that are sterile and controversial which, for the most part, are made for the common herd. These must be left to those who serve the public whose company they keep. Speaking personally, I only like books that are enjoyable or easy to read, books which hook my curiosity or console or counsel me on how to live and die,

Silently sauntering through salubrious groves, pondering on what is worthy of the man who is wise and good.

HORACE, *EPISTOLAE*, I, IV, 4

Wiser men, being possessed of souls that are strong and vigorous, can devise for themselves a restful form of peace which is wholly spiritual. But I, who have an ordinary soul, must stay myself with bodily pleasures and, since age has now robbed me of those which once were most to my fancy, I train and whet my appetite for those that remain and are more suitable to this than to the other seasons of my life. We must cling on with tooth and claw to the enjoyment of life's pleasures which the passing years wrest from our grip one after the other.

Let us reach out for life's sweetness; how you live is yours to choose. Soon you will be ashes, dust, a ghost, a subject for idle talk.

—PERSIUS, *SATIRÆ*, V, 151

As to fame and glory, the end which Pliny and Cicero recommend to us, they are far removed from my reckoning. Ambition is the humour that runs most contrary to retirement. Fame and private peace cannot lodge under the same roof. As I see it, arms and legs are all both those authors keep free of the herd; in reality, their hearts and souls remain more closely involved with it than ever.

So, Sir Greybeard, are you picking up tasty titbits to catch people's ears with?

—PERSIUS, *SATIRÆ*, I, 22

But all they do is step back to give themselves a clearer run and gain momentum to jump the ditch and land in the middle of the crowd.

But would you like to know just how far they fall short of the target? Let us set against them the view of two other philosophers of very different schools, writing to their friends, the one to Idomeneus and the other to Lucilius, urging them to retire to a quiet life by abandoning their public roles and high office.

'You have thus far,' they said, 'lived your lives swimming and floating on the surface. It is back to port that you must come to die. You have given the best of your life to the limelight: devote what is left to obscurity. It will be impossible to give up your activities unless you also give up their fruits. To this end, forget all thought of fame and honours. There is a danger that the glow of your achievements will continue to light you brightly and follow you all the way to the refuge to which you have retreated. When you renounce pleasure, include the warmth that comes from the good opinion of others. And as to your learning and independence of mind, fear not: they will not dim if you are made the wiser by them. Remember the man who, when asked what he was trying to achieve by working so hard at an art which could come to the notice of only a small number of people, replied: "I would be satisfied with those few," said he, "I would be content with just one and be happy with none."

'He spoke a truth: you and a single companion are sufficient audience for each other. Let your public be just one person or indeed let it be your own self. It is a poor sort of ambition that in your private retreat leads you to conceive hopes of a crown of laurels as a reward for your idleness. You must do as the animals do that hide their tracks at the entrance to their lairs. You should stop caring about how people talk about you, and care only about how you should talk to yourself. Withdraw into yourself but first prepare a welcome in the place where you will be received. It would be folly to put your fate in your own hands if you cannot govern yourself. A man may fail when he is alone as easily as he does when surrounded by others. Until such time as you succeed in becoming the kind of man in whose presence you would not like to slip up and blunder, and not before you have learnt to feel ashamed but also to respect yourself,

Let honest things be ever present in the mind

—CICERO, *TUSCULANÆ DISPUTATIONES*, II, XXII, 52

—and let your imagination dwell on the models of Cato, Phocion and Aristides in whose presence fools would always hide their faults. Make them the censors of your innermost thoughts which, if they stray, your deference to them will set to rights again. They will keep you on a path where you will be content with yourself, where you will borrow nothing from anyone but yourself and limit your soul to wholesome thoughts in which it will be at ease. And having acknowledged what are the true treasures which we will enjoy all the more the better we understand them, we shall be satisfied with them and not wish to prolong our lives or to want our name to live after us.'

That is the counsel of true and natural philosophy, not of some brash and boastful doctrine such as that of our first two schoolmen.

On the Uncertainty of Our Judgement

What this line of Homer's *Iliad* (XX, 249) says is indeed well said: 'The tongue has many words, and it is possible to speak for or against anything'. For example:

Hannibal won battles but did not win wars

—PETRARCH, *CANZONIERE*, 103

A man who took that view might use it to show our leaders that it was an error not to turn our recent victory at Montcontour to better account, or to accuse the King of Spain of not making the most of the advantage he had over us at Saint Quentin. But that same man might equally say that such failings spring from hearts intoxicated by heady good fortune and from minds which, glutted with a first taste of success, lose the appetite for more, being unable to digest what they have already been served with. The victors have their arms too full to hold any more triumphs and feel unworthy that

Fortune should have chosen to indulge them so. For what have they gained if they then hand their enemies an opportunity to regroup and recover? What hope is there that they will think to mount a fresh attack later, after their opponents have had time to rally, gather their forces and are newly primed with hate and a thirst for vengeance, if they did not dare to harry and chase them down when they were broken and terrified?

When fortune is roused and terror rules

—LUCAN, *PHARSALIA*, VII, 734

But all things considered, what better opportunity can the victors expect than the one they have just squandered? Warfare is very different from fencing where the number of hits clearly determines who wins, for as long as the enemy is still on his feet, everything is still to play for—and it is not victory unless it ends the war. In the skirmish where Cæsar came off badly before the city of Oricum, he criticized Pompey's soldiers, saying that he might have lost the encounter entirely if their commander had known how to press home a victory, and when he came up against Pompey again he made him spur his horse in a very different direction.

But why should we not say on the contrary that it is the effect of a hasty, covetous mind to refuse to place a limit on its coveting; that it is to abuse God's favour to exceed the temperate conduct which He prescribed for it; and that to slide carelessly back into danger after the victory is won is to leave victory at the mercy of Fortune; that one of the wisest rules of the military art is not to drive the enemy to the point of despair. Sylla and Marius in the Marsic War, having defeated the Marsi, saw one last remnant of troops who turned like enraged beasts, preparing to launch a final desperate attack against them, and were not minded to stand and wait for them to come on to them. If the ardour of Monsieur de Foix had not urged him to set off in hot pursuit of the survivors of the victory of Revenna, he would not have stained it with his own death. Yet the recent memory of his example served to preserve Monsieur d'Anguien from a similar fate at Cérisoles. It is dangerous to attack a man you have left with only one means of escape—his sword—for needs must when the devil drives:

When roused, necessity bites hardest

—Portius Latro

It will cost you dear to defeat a foe you provoke by saying you will cut his throat

—Lucan, *Pharsalia*, IV, 275

It is for that reason that Pharax prevented the King of Sparta, who had won the day against the Mantoneans, from going forth to confront a thousand Argians who had escaped unharmed from their loss, and persuaded him to let them leave unchallenged so that they would not try to prove their valour which had been goaded and inflamed by defeat.

After his victory, Clodomire, King of Aquitaine, going in pursuit of Gondemar, King of Burgundy, who he had vanquished and was fleeing, compelled him to turn and face him. But this obstinacy robbed him of the fruit of his victory, for he was slain on the spot.

Similarly, the man who had to choose either to keep his troops richly, superbly armed at all times or to arm them only when it was necessary would surely opt for the first—along with Sertorius, Philopœmen, Brutus, Cæsar and others—on the grounds that it is ever a spur to a soldier's honour and reputation to see himself bravely accoutred, as well as a means of making him more determined in combat by having to safeguard his weapons, which are the equivalent of his entire estate and inheritance. Xenophon says this was the reason why troops in Asian armies always took with them to war their wives and concubines, along with their jewels and richest possessions.

On the other hand, it could be argued that rather than encouraging the fighting man's concern with preserving his life, it would serve more purpose to wean him off it, as it will make him afraid to court danger on two counts: fear of death and loss of his equipment. Furthermore, the practice increases among the enemy's ranks the lust for victory and the rich booty that goes with it. On other occasions, it has been further noted that it wonderfully fired Roman soldiers when they fought the Samnites. When Antiochus showed Hannibal the army he had raised against the Romans, magnificently and gorgeously furbished with instruments of every kind, he asked him:

'And will my army be enough for the Romans?'

'Enough?' Hannibal replied. 'I should say so, however greedy they might be.'

Lycurgus ordered his men not only to avoid appearing conspicuously equipped but also to refrain from stripping the corpses of their defeated foes, wishing, he said, that poverty and frugality would shine brighter than anything else on the field of battle.

At sieges and other conflicts where events bring us close to our enemies, we happily give our soldiers their heads to defy, jeer and curse them with all kinds of insults and we do not do it without good reason. For it is no small matter to deprive our opponents of all hope of mercy or quarter by showing them that the foe that they have so sorely provoked cannot be expected to be magnanimous: there can be no salvation for them but victory. That was where Vitellius made his great mistake. For having to face Otho, who was the weaker because of the low fighting spirit of his soldiers who were long unaccustomed to warfare and enervated by the pleasures of Rome, he so goaded them with stinging taunts, accusing them of cowardice and mocking their mooning regrets for the fleshpots and women of the city, that he put fire in their bellies, which was more than all manner of urging had succeeded in doing, and roused them to close hard with his soldiers, a thing which their captains had been unable to achieve. For it is true that such insults, when they cut to the quick, are more than able to push the man who marches stolidly forth to defend his king's cause to quicken his pace, get his blood up and make the fight his own.

Considering how crucial it is to protect the life of the commander of an army and given the plain fact that the enemy's prime target is that one man on whom all the others lean and depend, you would think there could be no doubt of the value of the ploy, which we have seen used by numerous great generals, of dressing differently and adopting a disguise at the point where battle is joined. However, the disadvantage of this manner of proceeding is that it is no less fraught than that which they believe they avoid. For when a commander arrives and is not recognized by his own men, the courage he should give them by his presence and example can start to evaporate. Moreover, on not seeing his customary marks and insignia, they may think he is dead or, believing the day to be lost, that he has left the field.

If we look further, we learn from experience that it is sometimes the first stratagem that succeeds, sometimes the second. What happened to Pyrgus in the battle he fought against Levinus in Italy helps us to judge both sides of the argument. For, having decided to don the armour of Demoglacles and give him his own to wear, he most certainly saved his life but came close to succumbing to the other danger, that of losing the day. Alexander, Cæsar and Lucullus favoured marking their presence on the battlefield with rich armour and accoutrements in their own gleaming colours. Agis Agesilaus and the mighty Gilippus on the contrary went to war inconspicuously dressed and without imperial devices or embellishments of any kind.

Among other failings which were laid against Pompey's door at the battle of Pharsalia was his decision to bring his army to a complete halt and wait for the enemy to come to him. This was an error because (here I shall borrow Plutarch's words which carry so much more weight than mine) 'it weakens the violence which men running add to the opening clashes and thereafter destroys the momentum which normally—and more than anything else—makes the combatants more reckless, more ferocious in those first brutal hand-to-hand encounters and raises their courage with shouting and martial bustle; whereas waiting makes the hot blood of the receiving troops, as it were, run cold and to turn to ice.' That is what Plutarch said.

Yet if Cæsar had lost, it might just as well have been said on the contrary that the most solid, foursquare stance for a man is to stay erect, motionless and with his feet firmly planted on the ground; that when troops come to a complete stop they can marshal and save their strength for what is to come, thus gaining a great advantage over the men who charge at them and are already winded from having used up half their breath by running; and added to which that it is impossible for an army, being a body made up of many individuals, to spring instantly into furious action in one concerted movement without upsetting or breaking its battle order and preventing the fittest soldiers being already in the thick of it before their slower comrades can come up to them to give support.

In the shameful battle at Cunaxa between the two Persian brothers, Clearchus the Spartan, who commanded the Greek soldiers of Cyrus' faction, launched them on an orderly, leisurely charge. But when he was at about fifty paces' distance, he ordered them to a gallop, hoping that over this modest distance he could preserve their line and spare their breath, while still giving them the advantage of momentum for both themselves and their javelins and projectiles.

Others have settled these doubts with their own armies as follows: if the enemy is charging, stand your ground; if the enemy stands waiting for you, launch your charge.

When Charles V made his incursion into Provence, the French king was faced with a dilemma, namely, whether to go into Italy and face him there, or wait for him to come inside his frontiers. He thought hard about how advantageous it would be to keep his own territory clear and free of the tumult of war so that, with its might uncompromised, it would continue to supply his needs, as they arose, with men and money. But he reflected too that the demands of war necessarily force armies to lay waste to the country they move through, which is not something that can easily be sanctioned on our home ground; that the peasantry might not put up with the ravages committed by its own side any more meekly than those of their king's enemies, so that seditions and unrest might arise among us; further, that the licence to pillage and plunder at will, which cannot be permitted in our land, is a great compensation for the hardships of war to soldiers who, having no prospect of relief beyond their bare pay and finding themselves only a short distance from wives and homes, would be tempted to desert; that whoever orders the feast must pay the bill; that it is more exhilarating to attack than to defend; and that the shock to the system which follows the loss of a battle can be so violent that it is hard to stop it jolting and unsettling the entire body politic, for there is no passion more catching nor more persuasive than fear, nor any that spreads so fast; and finally that in the cities, which hear the din of havoc at their gates and let back in their generals and soldiers still shaking and panting for breath, there will be the danger, in the heat of that moment, that they will fall back upon some ill-advised course of action. Yet despite all these considerations, the king chose to recall his forces already deployed in the mountains of Italy, opting to wait for the enemy to come to him.

For he was well aware of the contrary argument that, being based in his own country and among friends, he could easily be fully provisioned with all manner of supplies, for the rivers and passes, being loyal to him, would safely bring victuals and money with no need of escorts; that he would have subjects whose affection for him would grow as the threat to them grew nearer; that having so many fortified towns and cities to guarantee his security, it would be for him to choose the time to fight when the moment was right and he had the most to gain; and if he chose to play for time, from the comfort of his base, he could watch while his enemies grew frustrated and weakened by the difficulties that beset them, being deployed in a hostile land where there was no one, no place that was not at war with them, not ahead of them, nor to their rear nor on either flank. They had no way of resting their men, of keeping them in isolation when disease came among them, or of providing shelter for their wounded; no money and no victuals save at the point of a lance; no time to rest and draw breath; no knowledge of either the terrain or the country which would enable them to be safe from ambush or surprise attack; and should it come to losing a battle, no way of recovering the remnants of their army.

There is no lack of examples to prop up both sides of this argument.

Scipio decided it was better to go to Africa and invade the lands of his enemy than to defend his own and fight him in Italy where he was at that time, and in this case things turned out very well for him. On the other hand, Hannibal during that same war was brought low because he abandoned his bid to conquer a foreign country and chose to return home and defend his own. The Athenians, having left their enemies in possession of their lands, passed into Sicily, but suffered badly at the hands of fate, which treated Agathocles, King of Syracuse, very differently, for he sailed away to Africa and left the war behind him at home.

And so we have grown used, with good reason, to saying that events and outcomes, particularly in matters of warfare, hang on the whims of Fortune which refuses to accept and abide by our reasoning and foresight, an idea expressed in the following lines:

> *Poor plans prevail where prudence fails. Fortune does not enquire into causes nor the merit of cases but flits at random. Clearly there is a higher will that rules us and decides the affairs of men according to its own laws.*

> —MANILIUS, *ASTRONOMICA* IV, 95

Yet if we read this aright it would seem that our deliberations and resolutions depend as much on Fortune as on anything else, but equally that Fortune also muddies our thinking with her uncertainties and confusions.

'All our deliberations,' said Plato's Timæus, 'are precarious and tentative because there is in our reckonings, as in ourselves, a strong element of chance.'

On Drunkenness

The world is nought but difference and dissimilarity. Vices are all alike only because they are vices and that is doubtless how the Stoics construed them. But though they may all be equally vices, they are not all equal vices. It is scarcely believable that the man who oversteps the limits by a hundred paces—

beyond and outside which right does not exist

—HORACE, *SATIRÆ*, I, I, 107

—can be deeper-dyed in vice than he who exceeds that mark by ten times, or that committing sacrilege is not worse than stealing a cabbage from my patch.

Reason will not persuade me that there is no more sin committed in uprooting tender plants in someone's garden than in stealing sacred objects at night.

—HORACE, *SATIRÆ*, I, III, 115

There is in fact as much difference between those two things as there is between any others.

Still, it is dangerous to confuse the order and magnitude of sins. Murderers, traitors, and tyrants benefit too much thereby. It is not right that their consciences are salved by comparison with others who are merely idle or lascivious or less than regular in their religious observance. Everyone comes down heavily on the sins of his neighbour and thereby minimizes his own. Even our religious leaders and directors often rank sins quite wrongly, to my mind.

Just as Socrates said that the first duty of wisdom is to distinguish good from evil, we (of whom even the best are touched by vice) should say the same of the business of differentiating between vices. If we do not make that clear, the virtuous and the sinful will remain much of a muchness and impossible to tell apart.

But compared to the rest of our vices, drunkenness stands out for me as being irretrievably gross and brutish. With all the other types, the mind retains a certain role and indeed there are vices which have something magnanimous about them, if I may express it so. There are some in which learning, dedication, valour, prudence, skill and subtlety play some part. But this vice of drunkenness is of the body and earthbound. Of the nations now which exist in the modern world, the least civilized of them is the only one where any good is said of it. The other vices may impair our understanding but drunkenness turns it on its head and makes the body slack and torpid.

When the power of wine starts to work in a man, his limbs grow heavy, he trips over his feet and staggers, his tongue grows thick, his brain becomes clouded, his eyes are bleary: he is all noise, hiccoughs and brawling

—LUCRETIUS, DE RERUM NATURA, III, 475

A man's lowest state is at the point where he loses consciousness and all control of himself.

And it is said, among other things, that as the must fermenting in a vessel causes whatever lies at the bottom to rise to the top, so wine wrests the most intimate secrets from the keeping of those who have drunk too much of it.

You, my wine-jug, reveal our cares and inmost thoughts to gleeful Lyacus [Bacchus]

—HORACE, ODES, XXI, 1, 114

Josephus tells how once, by giving him copious amounts to drink, he wormed the secrets out of a certain ambassador who had been sent to him by his enemies. Yet on the other hand, Augustus, having entrusted his most private thoughts to Lucius Piso, the conqueror of Thrace, was never failed by him; nor was Tiberius betrayed by Cossus, to whom he opened all his mind, though we know them both to have been so strongly given to wine that they often had to be carried out drunk from the Senate,

their veins still inflamed, as usual, with yesterday's drink.

—VIRGIL, ECLOGUES, V, 15

And the plot to kill Julius Cæsar was as safe when communicated to Cimber, who was known to be often drunk, as it was to Cassius, who drank nothing but water. On that occasion Cimber jested: 'Why should I go on carrying a tyrant when I cannot carry my wine?' And we see that our German mercenaries, though sodden with drink, always remember where their camp is, what the watchword is and their rank.

> *Nor does victory come easily even when the enemy are wine-soaked, babbling and falling-down drunk*

—JUVENAL, SATIRÆ, XV, 47

I should not have believed insobriety in anybody could be so utterly deep-seated, firmly rooted and entrenched had I not read the following in the history books: that Atalus, having invited to dinner, with a view to causing him severe embarrassment, the same Pausanius who, in connection with the incident, later slew Phillip, King of Macedon (a king who by his excellent qualities stood as witness to the education he had received in the house and company of Epaminondas), made him drink so much that he became stupefied to the point where he was prepared, not knowing what he did, to abandon his handsome body to muleteers and many of the grovelling servants of his household, as though it was the carcase of some country whore.

And then there is what I learnt from a lady whom I honour and most singularly esteem, that in the region of Bordeaux, near Castres where she has her house, a village woman, a widow, known for her chaste way of living, on feeling the first discomforts of pregnancy told her neighbours that she would truly believe she was with child if she still had a husband. But when day by day the evidence for her suspicion grew stronger and proved to be true, she was forced to have it announced from her parish pulpit that if the man responsible admitted the deed, she would forgive him and was, if he so wished, prepared to marry him. A young fellow who served her as a ploughman, emboldened by her declaration, came forward and stated that, one feast day, he had found her, after she had taken a great quantity of wine, so deeply asleep by her fireside and in so indecent a pose that he was able to take advantage of her without waking her. They still live together as man and wife.

It is quite clear that this vice was not roundly condemned in Antiquity. The writings of several philosophers speak of it but in only the mildest terms. And until the age of the Stoics, some sages even advised that on occasion we should give ourselves a licence to drink what we like and even to get drunk as a way of refreshing the soul.

> They say that in any trial of capacity, great Socrates often ran
> away with this prize too

—Pseudo-Gallus, I, 47

Cato the Elder, the Censor and reprover of others, was himself reproved for his taste for the bottle:

On Drunkenness

It is said of Old Cato that his fire was often stoked by wine.

—HORACE, ODES, XXI, III, II

Cyrus, that king of high renown, among the other praiseworthy attributes for which he reckoned he was to be preferred to his brother Ataxerxes, also claimed that he was the better drinker. Among the best regulated and governed nations, the test of assessing a man by how much he can drink has been widely in use. I have heard it said of Silvius, the eminent physician of Paris, that he would recommend, to promote strong digestion and prevent the stomach from growing lazy, that once a month we should arouse the digestive organ by excess of this sort so as to stop it growing sluggish. It is also written that the Persians would attend to their most important affairs after drinking.

But in truth my own taste and humour are much more opposed to this vice than my reason. For, setting aside my customary practice of submitting in my beliefs to the authority of the ancient authors, I regard this vice as craven and foolish but much less malignant and harmful than the rest which, almost without exception, do greater and more immediate damage to society at large. And if it is true, as my authors claim, that we can never allow ourselves a modicum of pleasure without regretting it in some way, then I will say that I find that wine pinches our conscience far less than the other vices do. Furthermore, it is a sin that is not hard to cater for and not difficult to procure—which is no small consideration.

A man well advanced in dignity and age once explained to me that of three great comforts that remained to him in life, drink was one of them. But he went about it the wrong way, for both delicate discrimination in taste and the worrisome business of choosing wines are to be avoided. If you set your pleasure on drinking the best, you will condemn yourself on occasion to having to drink the worst. Your taste should be less narrow, less fastidious. To be a good drinker, the palate should not be delicate. Germans drink almost any sort of wine with equal pleasure. Their aim is to quaff not taste. As a result, they are better served, for the supply of their pleasure is greater and more easily obtained.

Secondly, to drink in the French fashion, at only two meals and then only in moderation, out of fear for one's health, is inadequate to allow proper appreciation of the favours of the god. More time should be devoted to it and we need to work harder at it. The ancients spent entire nights applying themselves to it and often continued on into the next day. No, a man should draw up his daily consumption on a larger and sounder scale. In my time I have seen a noble lord, a personage of great enterprise and successful ventures, who, during the course of his regular meals, would easily empty perhaps five bottles of wine and, on rising from table, be only too self-possessed and shrewd in the conduct of our business.

Pleasure, which we would like to think of as something we can count on having all through life, should occupy a larger place in it. Like menials who serve us in shops and common labourers, we should not pass up any opportunity to imbibe but rather keep the thought of it always in our mind. Instead, it seems that we are reducing our consumption all the time. And in our houses, great dinners, copious luncheons and banquets once used to be much more frequent and common than they are at present, as I remember them from my childhood,

Does this mean that this is one area in which we are changing for the better? Absolutely not. The reason for it is rather that we are now more given to rutting than our forefathers were. In practice, here are two activities which cancel each other out. On the one hand, lechery weakens the digestion and, on the other, moderate drinking makes us more sportive and lusty for the business of love.

It is a matter of great wonder to me how many tales I heard my father tell of the chasteness of the times he lived in. He was well qualified to speak on the question being a handsome man and, both by his bearing and nature, most agreeable to the ladies. He spoke little but well and in his conversation made cultured reference to fashionable authors of the day, mainly Spanish, and among them made frequent allusion to the one entitled *Marcus Aurelio* [by Antonio de Guevara, 1528]. His demeanour was ever kindly, humble and unassuming but overall very sober. He took particular care to show himself open and honest in his person and dressed with suitable decorum both when on foot and on horseback. He was unusually true to his word once given and he was possessed of a conscience and a faith bordering on punctiliousness. Though a man short in stature, he was very strong and his figure was straight-backed and well-proportioned. His face was agreeable and tended to the swarthy and he was adroit and accomplished in all the noble exercises. I still have in my possession the lead-weighted canes which they say he used to exercise his arms for throwing the bar, putting the shot and fencing, and also shoes with lead soles which he wore to train himself up to run and jump. People still remember the miraculous way he performed at vaulting. When he was past sixty years of age, I recall how he scoffed at our sporting efforts and, still in the fur-lined gown he always wore, he would jump onto a horse or hop over a table resting only on his thumbs and he hardly ever went up to his chamber without taking the stairs three or four at a time.

But more to my point, he told me that of all the women of quality in the entire province there was scarce one who had a blot on her name and then proceeded to rattle through strange tales of men, including himself, who were on friendly terms with chaste women who were totally above suspicion. And with regard to his own case, he swore on his oath that he went to his marriage bed a virgin. He said he had seen long service in wars beyond the Alp mountains, of which he left, written in his own hand, a journal giving a point-by-point account of what had then transpired both in public and to him in private. As a result he married when he was no longer young, in the year 1528 (which was also his thirty-third) on his return from Italy.

But we have forgot our bottles.

The discomfitures of old age—which ever stands in need of shoring up and refurbishing—might well and legitimately prompt me to develop a taste for drink, since it is virtually the last of the pleasures that the passage of years robs us of. Regular drinkers reckon the natural heat of our thirst starts in the feet: it begins there in infancy. From there it rises up into the middle parts where it long resides and, in my view, yields the only true joys of our physical lives: next to it, all other pleasures are but half-delights. In time, like steam or vapour which float or drift upward, it reaches the throat where it comes to its final rest.

However, I do not understand how it is that we are able to prolong the pleasure of drinking beyond the slaking of our thirst, nor how in our imagination we can create an appetite that is artificial and quite unnatural. My belly could not manage the equivalent, being utterly prevented from further indulgence after it has taken in the full quotient of its needs. My constitution requires me not to think of drink except after eating, to wash the food down, and for that reason I make my last bumper the largest. Anarcharsis notes with surprise that the Greeks at the end of their meals drank from larger cups than at the start. It was, I think, also for that reason that the Germans do likewise and that is when they then begin the battle of who can drink the most.

Plato forbade children to taste wine before the age of eighteen, and men to get drunk before they are forty years of age. But once past that mark he gave them leave to please themselves and admit into their convivialities the influence of Dionysius, that kindly god who restores gaiety to adult men, youth to the old and mollifies and softens the passions of the soul as iron is made malleable by fire. In his *Laws,* Plato further extends his favour to drinking fellowships (provided there is always a residing president to supervise and keep order) which serve a useful purpose, intoxication being a pretty sure and accurate indicator of a man's character. But such institutes are also well-suited to giving older members the courage to make merry with dancing and music which are beneficial activities that they are less than likely to take up when sober. He also says that wine furnishes the spirit with equanimity and the body with sound health. However, he favoured certain restrictions in part borrowed from the Carthaginians: that wine should be used in moderation by men on active service in time of war; that lawmakers and official arbiters should abstain totally both when they discharge their court duties and deal with matters of public interest; that wine should be eschewed during the day, which is the time for other occupations, and indulged on nights when a man sets out to beget children.

It is said that the philosopher Stilpo, weighed down by his years, deliberately hastened his end by drinking his wine undiluted with water. The same cause, but not the same intention, also snuffed out the last of the strength of Arcesilaus.

But what of that old but intriguing question, namely whether the functioning capacities of a wise man can be overthrown by the power of wine?

Shall it break through wisdom's stout defences?

—HORACE, *ODES*, III, XXVIII, 4

On Drunkenness

To what high degree of inanity will the good opinion we have of ourselves not raise us? The best regulated head in the world is already hard put to keep its balance and stop itself being toppled to the ground by its own inadequacies. Out of a thousand minds there is not one that is capable of standing straight and upright for the space of one single minute of its life and it is doubtful, were it left to its natural inclinations, that it could ever be managed at all. But could we but add consistency of judgement to that straight uprightness, then the mind would indeed reach its ultimate perfection, by which I mean that nothing then would divert or deflect it, which is what a thousand freak or chance hazards regularly do. That great poet Lucretius can philosophize and puff himself up as much as he likes but lo! suddenly he is driven mad by a love potion. And do they seriously believe that an apoplectic fit will not deprive Socrates of his wits as easily as it will a street porter? Some people forget their own names in the wake of serious illness and a trifling injury has scattered the wits of others. A man may be as wise as he likes but in the end he is still a man—and what is there more impotent, more wretched or of less account than a man? Wisdom has no power over our physical being:

We see sweat and pallor spread over his body, his tongue is disabled and his voice cracks, his eyes darken, his ears ring, his limbs give way until he slumps to the ground as panic rises in his mind.

—Lucretius, *De Rerum Natura*, III, 155

105

When threatened, he cannot prevent his eyes shutting against the coming blow; he cannot stop himself trembling when he stands on the edge of a precipice, any more than a child could. For Nature chooses to retain these small marks of her authority, which ride roughshod over our reason and Stoic virtue, in order to remind man that he is mortal and a very foolish creature. He turns pale when afraid, he blushes when ashamed and when seized by the colic, he cries out in a voice which, when not desperate or stentorian, is broken and wheezy

He must understand that nothing human is foreign to him!

—TERENCE, *HEAUTONTIMORUMENOS*, I, i, 25

The poets, who dress up everything according to their fancy, do not dare to excuse their heroes their due of whimpering:

Thus [Aeneas] muttered through his tears and his fleet, unleashed, sailed away.

—VIRGIL, *ÆNEID*, VI, i

It is enough that a man should rein in and curb his feelings, because he has it not in him to suppress them altogether. Even our own Plutarch (so just and fine a judge of the actions of men) when he wrote of Brutus and Torquatus murdering their children, began to doubt if virtue could go that far and to wonder if instead those men had not been thrown off balance by some passion or other. All actions that fall outside the

On Drunkenness

ordinary norms are open to dark interpretations, for higher
things are no more to our liking than the lower sort.

Let us leave out of this reckoning the other clan [the Stoics]
who openly profess their haughty superiority. But when, even
from within the ranks of the tribe that is considered the more
indulgent [the Epicureans], we hear this boastful swaggering
from Metrodorus—

*Fortune, I have foiled and blocked you! I have barred all roads
that lead to me: you cannot hope to get close!*

—Cicero, *Tusculanæ Disputationes*, V, 9

—or when Anaxarchus, by the decree of Nicocreon, tyrant of
Cyprus, was laid in a giant stone mortar and beaten to death
with an iron-clad pestle, he continued to repeat over and over:
'Strike! Lay on! 'tis not Anaxarchus you hammer but the outward husk of him!'; and when we hear our Christian martyrs
from the midst of the flames call out to the Tyrant: 'This side
is well done, cut slices and eat, for it is fine roasted—and then
you can make a start on the other side!'; and when we read in
Josephus of the boy shredded by the biting tongs and pierced
all through by the gimlets of Antiochus and how he still defied
him, crying out in a voice that was calm and assured: 'Tyrant,
you labour in vain! I am still here and still feel no pain! Where
is the agony, where the torments you threatened to rain down
on me? Is this the best you can do? My steadfast faith hurts
you more than your cruelty hurts me: Ah! craven varlet, you
gnash your teeth and I grow stronger! Make me scream with

agony, make me bend, make me yield if you can. Rally your henchmen and spur on your hangmen, for they are losing heart and have come nearly to the end of their armoury of horrors. Give them new tools! Unleash their ferocity!'—then in truth, we must admit that such souls undergo a change for the worse, and that some frenzy—albeit holy—must surely possess them.

When we encounter the provocations of the Stoics, such as 'I would rather be furiously mad than lasciviously bad' (one of Antisthenes' sayings) or when Sextius tells us that he would prefer to be in the grip of pain rather than of lust; and when Epicurus decides to make light of his gout and, refusing to both rest and take care of his health, cheerfully scoffs at all ailments, dismissing minor pains and, even as he disdains to resist and combat them, calls instead for others which are agonizing and excruciating and thus more worthy of him—

> *Among his peaceful herd, he hopes that some boar or tawny lion*
> *will descend from the mountain*

—Virgil, *Æneid*, IV, 158

—who, I ask, would not conclude that such words are the blustering bravado of a mind that has drifted free of its moorings? The soul could not both remain in her natural place and fly so high. To do that, she must needs break out, rise on the wind and, taking the reins between her teeth, seize and carry her man off over so great a distance that afterwards he is amazed by what he has done. It is what happens in time of war, when the heat of battle may push brave soldiers to perform actions so dangerous that when they are themselves once more, they are the first to be struck by the wonder of it. The same is true of poets who are often filled with amazement at their own writings and no longer know what path they followed to bring off their finest achievements. At such times, they too are visited by what is called frenzy or exaltation. And as Plato says, a man of settled, sober outlook will gain nothing by knocking on the door of poetry. Aristotle also takes the view that no sane mind is without a streak of madness and is right to apply the word to any transport or exalted state—however laudable it might be—which goes beyond our reason and our settled opinion of things. For wisdom is the well-regulated working of the soul, which it guides with measure and proportion and answers for it.

Plato argues as follows: that the gift of prophecy comes from on high and that we must be out of ourselves when we attempt it. Our customary circumspection must be lulled either by sleep or sickness, or else be raised free of its natural setting by a visitation of rapture from heaven above.

PART THREE

On Governance and Governors

Montaigne's scattergun approach to intellectual enquiry made room for a range of ethical problems, but also included more specific topics such as education or, in his century of conquest, colonialism. But having been an officer of the Parlement of Bordeaux and later, for two terms, its mayor, he acquired a practical understanding of administration, high politics, the workings of the law and the nature of power. His personal experience, backed as always by his reading of ancient authors, led him to consider a range of social and political issues, such as the shape and goals of a just society, the proper exercise of power and the duties of rulers.

12

On Cannibals

When King Pyrrhus crossed into Italy and surveyed the well-marshalled disposition of the army which the Romans had sent to face him: 'I do not know,' he said, 'what barbarians are these' (this was the name the Greeks gave to all foreigners) 'but there is nothing barbaric about the deployment of the army which I see there.' The Greeks said as much of the force which Flaminius led into their domains, as also did Phillipus, observing from a hilltop the disciplined order of the Roman encampment established in his kingdom by Publius Sulpicius Galba. This goes to show that we should guard against clinging to received opinions and instead judge with the eyes of reason and not trust to the common view.

I once had in my service for some time a man who had lived for ten or a dozen years in that other—New—world which was discovered in our century, at the same place [in Brazil] where Villegagnon made landfall and called *Antarctic* France. The discovery of a country of limitless extent seems to me a considerable matter. I do not know if I can say for sure that another discovery of this sort might yet be made, since many men greater than I have been mistaken in such speculation. I fear we have eyes that are bigger than our bellies and that our curiosity is greater than our understanding. We clutch at everything but catch only wind.

Plato calls on Solon to relate how he was told by the priests of Saïs in Egypt that in former times, before the Flood, there was a great island called Atlantis, which stood at the mouth of the Strait of Gibraltar, that contained more countries than Africa and Asia combined and that the Kings of that great realm possessed not only the Island but had spread their dominion so far over the continental mainland that they were masters of the breadth of Africa clear away to Egypt, and of the length of Europe down to Tuscany and that they had further undertaken to hop across into Asia and subjugate all the nations that border the Mediterranean even unto the Black Sea. To this end, they overran all parts of Spain, Gaul, Italy and reached Greece, where the Athenians resisted them. But some time later, the Athenians and they, together with their Island, were swallowed up by the Flood. It is quite likely that this mighty tide of water left the settled face of the earth very much altered, for it is said that the sea then divided not only Sicily from Italy—

> *those lands, they say, that once were joined long ago, were riven*
> *by a huge and violent convulsion and torn apart*

—VIRGIL, *ÆNEID*, III, 414

—but also Cyprus from Syria, the Isle Euboea from the *terra firma* of Boeotia and elsewhere, but also joined together lands hitherto divided, filling the trenches separating them with alluvium and sand:

> *The marsh so long uncultivable and navigable by oarsmen now feeds cities and bears the weight of the plough.*

> —HORACE, *ARS POETICA*, V, 65

But there is no likelihood that the Island we speak of is this same New World which we have just discovered, for it was almost in touching distance of Spain and it would be an inconceivable effect of the Flood to have moved it to where it now is, more than twelve hundred leagues away. Moreover, the voyages of modern navigators have more or less established that it is not an island but dry land, a continent, having India to one side and on the other the lands that lie below the two poles; or if it indeed is separated from them, then it is by such a narrow channel that it cannot on that account really be called an island.

It would seem that these great land bodies are subject, just as are our own, to pressures—some natural and others erratic. When I consider the changes my Dordogne river has made in my lifetime to the right bank of its downward course and reflect that in twenty years it has eaten away so much of it and washed away the foundations of several buildings, I see very clearly that it has, at some point, experienced some unusual kind of disruption. Because if it had always behaved in this way, or if it continues to do in future, the lie of the land would be very different. But rivers are subject to change, at times overflowing this way, sometimes that and at others not overflowing at all. I am not talking about sudden floods, the local cause of which we can readily account for. But in the Médoc, my brother, the Sieur d'Arsac, has seen a part of his estate that borders the shore buried under sand spewed up by the sea and through it the tops of some buildings still show. His rental income has dried up and his fields become arid grazing. The local people say that for some time past the sea has been encroaching on them so strongly that they have lost four leagues of land to it. The dunes are like a corps of vanguard troops: great mounds of moving sand driven by the waves advancing half a league and covering the land.

The other piece of evidence from antiquity on which the discovery of the New World may have some bearing is found in Aristotle—if, that is, a short work entitled *Marvels Beyond Belief* was in fact written by him. He tells how a number of Carthaginians, having set out to cross the Atlantic Sea through the Strait of Gibraltar, had in due course discovered, at a great distance from any continental land, a large, fertile island entirely covered with trees and watered by wide, deep rivers. Attracted by the excellence and fertility of the soil, they, like others after them, emigrated with their wives and children and began a settlement there. The Lords of Carthage, seeing the population of their country decline little by little, expressly forbade any more of them to leave, on pain of death, and also drove out those who had newly settled there lest, so it was said, in the fullness of time, they so multiplied in number that they outgrew the mother population and brought about the ruin of the state.

This account by Aristotle has no relation to our New World either.

Now, the man in my service was a simple, rough and ready sort, qualities which made him the kind best fitted to give trustworthy reports. While clever people have more curiosity and notice more, they put a gloss on things and, to impose their views and convince, cannot help altering what they report. They do not give you the picture penny-plain but put a slant on it and mask the face of what they saw. To lend weight to their view and persuade you to accept it, they show their side of the picture, amplify and spin it out. What is needed is either a man who speaks the plain truth or one so simple that he is incapable of embroidering or giving plausibility to tall tales and has no particular axe to grind. My fellow was just such a man. In addition to this, he introduced me at various times to various sailors and merchants he had met on his voyage hence. And so I am happy to accept his evidence without looking into what the cosmographers say on these matters.

We need topographers to provide accurate descriptions of the places they have themselves visited. But because they have had the privilege of a voyage to Palestine, they use that fact to feel qualified to tell us about the rest of world. I would much prefer it if people wrote down what they know and as much as they know—and not merely in this but on all other subjects too. Thus a man may well have some special knowledge or experience of the nature of some river or spring but otherwise know no more about things in general than anyone else. Yet to launch this small wisp of knowledge, he will produce an entire treaty of physics. From this failing stem a great many problems.

But to return to my subject. In all the reports I have been given of this new nation, I find nothing in it that is barbaric or wild except the fact that people call 'barbaric' anything they are not used to. For it seems that the only standard we have of truth and reason is the example and rationale of the customs and practices of the country in which we live, where we believe the form of religion is perfect, the form of government is perfect and the way everything is managed is advanced and perfect. But these other peoples are wild in the sense that we say that the fruits of nature, produced through her ordinary processes, are wild, whereas it is really those fruits which we have artificially modified and deflected from the natural order that we should rightly call wild and 'savage'. The former are vivifying and vigorous; they are the true, the useful, inborn essences and attributes, which we have denatured and adulterated, merely appropriating them to suit our corrupt taste. And yet our taste still finds that flavour and delicacy excellent, the envy of our own, when we eat various fruits from those countries where they are produced without benefit of agriculture. It is not reasonable that our ingenuity should be held in greater esteem than our great and mighty mother Nature. We have so overloaded the beauty and riches of her handiwork with our interference that we have totally suffocated her. In reality, in everything where her pure light still shines, she puts our vain and feeble works to shame.

> *Ivy grows best when left to itself, the strawberry tree thrives untended in shady hollows and the song of birds is sweeter for being untaught.*

—Propertius, *Elegiæ*, I, ii, 10–12

Our very best efforts do not come close to building the nest of the smallest bird, to replicating its construction, beauty and its perfect fitness for its purpose, no more than we can duplicate the web of the humble spider. All things, said Plato, are made by nature or chance or human contrivance; the greatest and fairest of them by one or other of the first two, and the least important and most imperfect by the third.

It is in this sense that these new nations seem 'barbarous' to me and, having been virtually untouched by the hand of man, they remain close to their primitive innocence. They are still ruled by the laws of nature and remain only lightly influenced by ours. Yet I grow vexed at times that our knowledge of that innocence did not come to us earlier, at a time when there were men better able to understand its significance than we are. It pains me that Lycurgus and Plato knew nothing of it, for it seems to me that what we see now of these new peoples, with the benefit of our experience, far exceeds not only the word-pictures with which poetry has embellished the supposed Golden Age but also the rosy tales which give a false idea of the happiness of man's original condition, and even the status of—and the enthusiasm for—philosophic thinking. Such writers simply could not conceive of a state of such pure and simple innocence such as we have come to see in the light of our discoveries; nor could they believe that a society can maintain itself with so little human interference and tinkering. To Plato, I say: here is a nation in which there is no kind of commerce, no knowledge of writing, no science of numbers, no title of ruler nor form of political hierarchy, no system of service, wealth or poverty, no contracts, no inheritance, no ownership of land, no occupations save the activities of leisure, no respect for kin except for the fellowship of the group, no clothes, no agriculture, no metal, no consumption of wine or cereals. Words that mean lie, treachery, deceit, avarice, envy, denigration, forgiveness do not exist there. Would he not find that his Republic falls far short of such perfection? Here are those 'men come fresh from the gods' of Seneca (*Epistolæ, XC, 44*) and 'these the manners first taught by nature' (Virgil, *Georgics*, II, 20).

Furthermore, they live in a most agreeable and temperate country so that, as I gather from my informants, it is rare to come across a man there who is ill. They also say that they saw no one who was feverish, rheumy-eyed, toothless or weighed down by age. They are settled by the sea, backed on the land side by great, high mountains, on terrain some hundred leagues wide. They have an abundance of fish and game which are nothing like ours and these they eat without other culinary attentions but the plain cooking of them.

The first man who rode a horse among them struck them with such terror that, though he had had dealings with them before on several other voyages, they riddled him with arrows before they could recognize him. Their dwelling houses are very long and able to accommodate two or three hundred souls. They are sheathed with bark and built with the trunks of great trees set on end in the ground which support each other by being inclined together and tied at their crowns, in the manner of certain of our barns, with the branches hanging down to the earth and serving as side-walls. They have a kind of wood so hard that they use it to make swords and the griddles on which they roast their meat. Their beds are made of cotton tissue and are slung from the roof like the hammocks of sailors on a ship, and each man has his own, for the women sleep apart from their husbands. They rise with the sun and once up immediately eat enough to last them all day; they have no other meal but that. At that time they do not drink, as Suidas remarks of several peoples in the Orient who drink only when not eating, for they drink several times during the day, and then do not stint themselves. Their drink is made from a particular root and is the colour of our clarets. They always drink it lukewarm because it does not keep for more than two or three days. It has a somewhat sharp taste, is not heady, is easy on the stomach and lenitive to those not used to it and a most agreeable drink to those who are. Instead of bread they use some kind of white pap resembling a mash of coriander. I have tried it. It tasted sweetish and rather bland.

Their entire day is spent dancing. The young men go out hunting for wild animals with bows and arrows. Some of the women, however, pass the time preparing their drink, this being their main employment. In the morning before they eat, one of the elders addresses the entire complement of the dwelling-house, walking from one end of it to the other repeating the same sentence over and over until he has completed his round, for those buildings are more than a hundred yards long. He enjoins them to observe only two precepts: courage in the face of their enemies and kindness to their wives. And the refrain never fails to exhort the men to observe this second duty to the women who ensure that their drink is kept warm and properly seasoned. The design of their beds, ropes, swords and the kind of wooden wrist armour which they wear in battle, plus the long canes, open at one end, whose sound sets the rhythm for their dances, are to be seen in many other lands and even in my own house. They are completely shaven, barbering themselves much more neatly than we do with razors made only from wood or stone. They believe that souls are immortal, and that those which have pleased the gods are given lodging in that part of the heavens where the sun rises and those that are cursed, in the west.

I have no idea what manner of priests and prophets they have but they come down at rare intervals from their mountain fastnesses and appear before the people. Whenever they come there is feasting and a general gathering of several villages (a barn, as I have already said, constituting a village, and villages being approximately one French league apart). Their prophet addresses them in public, exhorting them to virtue and duty; but their entire ethical doctrine is made up of the same two precepts, staunchness in war and love for their wives. He tells of things which are to be, of the outcomes which they may expect for their undertakings, and incites them to war or turns them away from it. But should he fail in his prognostications and the future turns out to be other than he predicted, then if they catch him he is found guilty of false prophesy and hacked into a thousand pieces. Which is why, if he has miscalculated, he is never seen again.

Divination being a gift of God, it is right, when it is abused, that it should be seen a punishable form of deception. Among the Scythians, when soothsayers failed in their prophesying, they were laid, feet and hands shackled, on ox-drawn carts filled with brushwood and burnt. Those who dabble in matters at the limit of human competence are excusable if they do their best. But what of those who peddle reassurance by trumpeting some extraordinary gift that is beyond our understanding? Should they not be punished both for failing to deliver what they promise and for the sheer cynicism of their quackery?

These people wage wars against nations whose lands lie further inland, on the far side of the mountains. They go naked into battle and have no weapons except bows and lengths of wood sharpened at one end like the heads of our boar spears. Their fighting spirit is remarkable and combat invariably ends in bloodshed and death, for they do not know the meaning of retreat and fear. Each victor brings back the head of an enemy he has slain as a trophy, and hangs it by the door of his lodge. They treat prisoners well for some considerable time and provide them with all the amenities they can think of. Then each man who has a prisoner calls a great assembly of his friends. He ties a rope around the arm of his captive and, grasping the end of it, holds him fast but out of his reach for fear of being set upon, then gives the other arm to his closest friend to hold in the same way. Then, with the entire company looking on, they hack him to pieces with their swords. When this has been done, they roast him. All present eat him up and send out slices and rashers to friends who are not there. This is not done, as might be thought, to feed themselves in the manner of the Scythians of old but as a symbolic representation of extreme revenge. This they do having observed that the Portuguese, who had made alliances with their enemies, had a different method of execution when they themselves were taken prisoner. This consisted of burying them up to the waist and shooting many arrows into them after which they hanged them. They believed that these invaders had come from the Other World (like others of their kind who had already spread knowledge of many vices among their neighbours), and that they were much greater masters than they in the practice of every kind of cruelty and did not use that form of revenge without some purpose of intimidation. They resolved that their own way with prisoners should be even more violent, so began to leave off their own ancient custom and adopted this new one.

I do not apologize for drawing attention to the barbarity of such a practice, but it would sadden me if, on hearing of it, we should judge their wickedness severely and be blind to our own. I think that there is more barbarity involved in eating a man alive, than when he is dead; in breaking his body with torture and racks when it is still capable of feeling pain; in allowing him to be bitten and savaged by dogs and boars (as we have not only read of but can ourself recall seeing enacted not between enemies long ago but by neighbours and fellow-citizens who, what is worse, did it in the name of piety and religion), than, in short, roasting him first and eating him when he is dead.

Chrysippus and Zeno, leaders of the Stoic sect, were both convinced that there is no wrong in making use of cadavers for whatever our needs may require, even down to using them for food—as when our ancestors, besieged by Cæsar in the city of Alexia, resolved to ease the hunger caused by their confinement with the bodies of the old, women and other persons unable to take up arms.

> *They also say that the Basques prolonged their lives by eating such food.*
>
> —JUVENAL, *SATIRÆ*, XV, 93

Nor do our physicians balk at using corpses for all kinds of applications, both internal and external, in the best interests of our health. But there has never been a point of view so extreme that has sought to excuse treachery, betrayal, tyranny, cruelty, which are our most common failings.

So we can call those peoples 'barbarians' only if we judge by the objective standard of reason, but not by comparison with ourselves who far surpass them in all manner of barbarous conduct. Their warfare is wholly fine and noble and has as much justification and splendour as that human sickness ever has: for them it has no other point than the defence of their honour. They do not go in quest of new lands to conquer because they already freely enjoy the abundance of nature without having to work or worry and do not need to extend their borders. They are still at that blessed stage of wanting no more than their natural needs require, anything more being superfluous.

They generally use the word 'brother' for those who are their own age; 'child' for those who are younger; while they all call old men 'father'. The latter bequeath to their heirs-in-common joint ownership of all their worldly goods, without any other title or authorization than that which nature confers on all its creatures when it brings them into the world.

If their neighbours cross the mountains to attack them and are victorious, the reward of the victors is their victory, the knowledge that they emerged the masters in valour and virtue. But that is all, for they have no interest in the possessions of the vanquished and in due course return to their own country where they want for nothing and do not lack that great boon: the gift of enjoying what they have and of being content with it. However, they then in turn do the same: they demand from their prisoners no other ransom than to admit and acknowledge that they were vanquished. But there is not one in a century who would not rather die than give an inch and, with a look or a word, defame the greatness of his invincible courage. There is not a man among their captives who would not prefer to be killed and eaten than to plead to be spared. They leave them some degree of freedom so that their lives can become dearer to them, and often they taunt them with their prospective death, the agonies they will suffer, the preparations being made for what awaits them, of the way their limbs will be lopped off and the feasting for which they will foot the bill. All this is done with the sole purpose of extracting a compliant or submissive word from them or of making them attempt to escape, so that the captors triumph at having made them feel afraid and broken their spirit. And here too, come to think of it, is the true essence of victory:

> There is no victory when the vanquished do not concede and admit defeat.
>
> —Claudian, *De Sexto Consulatu Honorii*, v. 248

The Hungarians of yore, so belligerent in war, would put up their swords once they had made the enemy beg for mercy. For having dragged this admission from them they let them go without further violence or ransom, and at most made them swear that they would never again take up arms against them.

As for us, the advantages we have over our enemies are borrowed and not truly our own. It is the attribute of a common porter, not of Valour, to have stronger arms and more powerful legs. Agility and dexterity too are natural, physical gifts, but in combat it is chance which causes your opponent to trip or be dazzled by the sun. Knowing how to handle a sword is entirely a product of training, an acquired skill which is available to any cowardly, worthless individual. The measure and worth of a man are defined by his heart and will: therein lies his honour. Courage is not strong arms and legs but inner fortitude; our valour is not defined by the bravery of our horse or the excellence of our weapons. He who falls in battle still firm of purpose and 'will yet, though his legs fail him, fight on his knees' (Seneca, *De Providencia*, II); he who knows he is about to die and does not flinch in his courage; he who as he dies stares back at his enemy with fierce, disdainful eyes—that man is beaten not by human hands but by fortune: he is killed but not conquered.

The bravest are sometimes the unluckiest.

There are defeats which are triumphs as great as any victory. The four related victories, the finest on which the Sun ever looked down, of Salamis, Plataea, Mycale, and Sicily, could never dare compare their combined glory with that of King Leonidas and his men at the pass of Thermopylæ.

Who ever went to war with a more glorious and greater lust for victory than Captain Iscolas, who yet lost his battle? Who ever devised more ingenious ways to assure his safety, than he did to assure his death? He was ordered to defend a pass in the Peloponnese against the Arcadians. Finding himself unable to do so given the nature of the terrain and uneven distribution of woodland cover, he concluded that none of the men who faced the enemy would ever leave the place alive; but considering it beneath his honour, a betrayal of his noble heart and of the name of Sparta, to fail in his mission, he chose a middle way between those two extremities which was as follows. He held back the youngest and fittest of his platoon, saving them for the future service and defence of their country, and sent them home. Then he thought how best to hold the pass with those whose loss would matter less, but who in dying would make the enemy pay for their passage as dearly as possible. And so it proved. Surrounded on all sides by Arcadian troops, he and his men made them pay a terrible price but he and they were all put to the sword. Was there a trophy awarded to a conqueror that was not more deserved by those who were conquered on that day? When properly understood, true victory is the combat, not survival. Valour lies in battling well, not battling through.

But to return to our tale, the prisoners, despite all that is done to them during the two or three months of their captivity, are nowhere near giving in but on the contrary continue to remain in good heart. They pester their captors to bring forward the day of their ordeal, they provoke them, insult them, accusing them of cowardice and reminding them of all the battles they have lost in past encounters with their countrymen. I have the words of a song written by one prisoner in which there is a passage where he invites them to step up, gather round and make a meal of him, for when they eat him they will be eating their fathers and grandfathers who fed and nourished his body.

'These muscles,' he says, 'this flesh, these veins are yours, poor fools that you are! Don't you recognize the flesh of your ancestors which still survives in them? Take time to savour them, for you will find they taste of your own flesh!'

I call that a broadside that can in no way be called barbaric. Artists who show them dying and being executed portray them spitting at their killers and poking out their tongues at them. They continue to defy them with words and looks until the moment when they draw their very last breath. Now that, compared to our ways, makes those men savages because, by our standards, if they are not wholly savage, then we must be. There is a huge distance between their customs and ours.

Their men have several wives, as many as is consistent with their standing and valour. It is a remarkable and admirable feature of their form of marriage that the jealousy which makes our wives hostile to their husbands' tender friendships with other women is among them an equal feeling in their favour. Being more attentive to their husbands' reputation than to anything else, they devote their best efforts to devising ways of finding as many wives for them as they can, as their number is an eloquent tribute to their husbands' manliness.

Our spouses would say this is monstrous, but it is not so. It is truly matrimonial, and in the highest sense. In the Bible, Sarah and Jacob's wives, Leah and Rachel, supplied their husbands with their serving-girls, and Livia preferred endorsing the appetites of Augustus in her own interest. Stratonice, wife of King Dejotarus, not only gave her husband the use of a very beautiful young chambermaid who served her but carefully raised the resulting children herself and backed them to succeed to their father's royal lands.

To avoid giving the impression that all this is done merely out of some routine or slavish observation of convention, or because it has the stamp of the authority of ancient practice, without being given any thought or justification because they are so dull of mind that they can think of no alternative, we should indicate a few facts in their defence. As well as the example I quoted from one of their war-chants, I have another, a love song, which starts like this:

'Halt, O Snake, do not move, Snake! so that my sister may use the pattern of your skin to design and make a rich girdle for me to give to my love. Do it, and your beauty and your markings will for ever set you above all other serpents.'

These opening lines are the refrain of the song. Now I have had enough truck with poetry to be able to form a view of this and I judge that not only is there nothing barbaric in the imagining of it but that it is perfectly Anacreontic. Their language, moreover, is soft-spoken and easy on the ear, with word-endings reminiscent of Greek.

Three men of that nation, not suspecting what a toll their introduction to our corrupted world would take on their happiness and peace of mind, and not yet knowing that they would be finally ruined by their dealings with us (though I suspect they were already well advanced down that road), and become very wretched at having let themselves be led on by the lure of novelty for which they had exchanged the calm skies of home to come and see ours—three of them, I say, were in Rouen in the time when the late Charles IX [then aged 12] was there. The king talked with them at length and they were shown our ways, our ceremonials and the shape and form of a fine city. Afterwards, they were asked for their opinion and to say what had impressed them most. They gave three answers, and I am very cross with myself for forgetting the third of them. But two have stayed in my memory. First, they said that they found it passing strange that so many tall, strong, bearded men in full armour who had surrounded the king (it is likely they meant the Swiss soldiers of his body-guard) should submit to obeying a boy instead of choosing one of themselves as a leader. Secondly, (and it is a particular feature of their language that they call all men the 'half' of one another) they said they had noticed that among our people were men who were fat and bloated with delicacies of every kind, while their other 'halves' were beggars at their doors, all skin and bones from hunger and poverty, and thought it strange that those penniless 'halves' should put up with such injustice and not grab the others by the throat or burn their houses down.

I spoke to one of them at length, but I had an interpreter who performed so badly for me and could not grasp my thoughts because he was so stupid, that I found very little joy in the conversation. When I asked my man what reward his rank among his people brought him (for he was a captain and our sailors called him a king), he said it was to march at the head of his troops into war. When I asked how many men were under his command he pointed to an area of ground, meaning as many as could fill that space, which could be in the order of four or five thousand. When I asked if his authority lapsed when there was no war, he said that enough of it remained that when he visited villages which were dependent on him, the villagers cut trails through their hedges and woods so that he could travel unhindered.

All this is not bad, not bad at all—ah yes, but *those people don't wear breeches…*

I 3

On the Inequality That Exists Between Us

Plutarch observes somewhere that he could see no more difference between one beast and the next than he found between one man and another. He was speaking of mental capacity and of inherent qualities. But I find Epaminondas, as I imagine him to have been, so far removed from any I have known and believed to be men of good sense, that I would go further than Plutarch. I would contend that there is more difference between one man and another than there is between a man and a beast of the field.

Ah, how superior is one man to another!

—Terence, *Eunuchus*, II, ii, I

I would add further that there are as many and as innumerable degrees of intelligence as there are fathoms of distance between the ground and the sky above.

But in this business of appraising and judging men, it is

amazing to think that, apart from ourselves, everything else is valued solely for its innate qualities. We admire a horse because it is strong and sure-footed—

> *We applaud the fleet steed that easily wins the palm of victory amid the cheers of the entire arena*
>
> —JUVENAL, SATIRÆ, VIII, LVII

—not for its harness; a greyhound for its speed, not for its collar; a falcon for its wings, not for its jesses and bells. Why do we not judge a man by his own natural worth? He may be a man of substance, with a fine palace, considerable standing and a large income, but all that is external to him and not his essence. You would not buy a pig in a poke, so if you are negotiating for a horse, you should take off its blanket and saddle and view it bare and uncovered. Or if it is paraded in with a handsome blanket thrown over it, as in olden times when horses were offered for sale to Kings and their caparison hid their least impressive points, you should not waste time admiring the blanket or the size of its hindquarters but concentrate mainly on legs, eyes and hooves which are the parts that matter most.

> *This is the way with kings when they buy horses: they inspect them covered, so that if, as is often the case, an attractive face diverts the eye from hooves that are soft and weak, it will not distract the buyer and encourage him to linger over a comely rump, a neat head and a handsome neck.*
>
> —HORACE, SATIRÆ, I, II, 86

Why, when you size up a man, do you measure him fully wrapped, like a parcel? All he lets us see are outward aspects of his person which have very little connection with him, while he hides those parts by which we might judge and assess his real worth. It is the quality of the sword that you should look for, not the fineness of the sheath. If you removed it from its scabbard you would probably not give a brass farthing for it. A man must be judged for what he is, not by his accoutrements. And as one ancient author amusingly put it, 'What makes you think that this fellow is tall? You've measured him with his built-up shoes on!' The plinth is not part of a statue: measure him with his high heels off. He must leave his wealth and honours in the cloakroom and appear for examination in just his shirt. Has he the physique he needs to carry out his functions? What sort of a soul does he have? Is she fine, capable and in full working order? Has she been enriched through her own efforts or are her riches borrowed? Has luck had anything to do with it? Would she look unflinchingly down the length of a drawn sword? Is she not indifferent to whether her life's last breath will escape as a weary sigh through the mouth or as a gasp from a slit throat? Is she serene, equable and content—these are the things that must be assessed and they are what we must use to judge the huge differences that exist between us.

The wise man who is master of himself, who fears nought from poverty, death and slavery, who commands his passions and spurns ambition, is that man not sufficient unto himself? Is he smooth, like a polished sphere to which nothing clings and by which even Fortune is rebuffed?

—HORACE, *SATIRÆ*, VII, 83-8

Such a man stands five hundred cubits above kingdoms and dukedoms. He is an empire unto himself:

The man who is wise is the master of his fate.

—PLAUTUS, *TRINUMMUS*, II, II, 84

What is left that he could possibly want?

For surely we see that human nature asks for nothing except a body free of suffering and peace of mind untouched by worry and fear.

—LUCRETIUS, *DE RERUM NATURA*, II, 16

Compare such a sage with today's race of men who are stupid, vulgar, servile and constantly buffeted by storms of motley passions which drive them this way and that while yet leaving them dependent on other people, and you will find they are further from each other than heaven is from earth. And yet the blindness of our ways is such that we take little or no account of all that when we compare a peasant and a king, a noble and a serf, a law-giver and a private citizen, a rich man and a pauper. For what strikes us at once is their extreme dissimilarity, although in fact they differ only, you might say, in the kind of breeches that they wear.

In Thrace, the king was distinguished from his people by a practice that was amusing but also excessive. He had his own religion, a god all to himself, which his subjects were not allowed to worship. This god was Mercury. He, for his part, scorned theirs: Mars, Bacchus and Diana.

But all such surface distinctions are cosmetic only, for they paint over the real differences. You see actors in a theatre portraying Kings or Emperors on stage, but when you see them again soon after, you also see them restored to their true and original condition of wretched valets and common coachmen. So it is with the emperor whose outward pomp so dazzles you

> *because he sports great emeralds set in gold which sparkle green fires and is meticulously dressed in a sea-blue robe of silk worn and stained with sweat from his bouts with Venus.*

> —LUCRETIUS, *DE RERUM NATURA*, IV. 1123

But look behind the curtain and what you see is just an ordinary man and no better than the least of his subjects—

> *the one is blessed in his inward self; the happiness of the other is fake*

> —SENECA, *EPISTOLÆ*, 119, 12

—because cowardice, lack of resolve, ambition and rancour torment him as much as any other man.

*For neither treasures nor being right hand to a Consul are enough
to ease the wretched tumults of his mind nor shut out the cares
that flit about beneath coffered ceilings*

—HORACE, *ODES*, II, XVI, 9

Even when surrounded by his battalions, anxiety and fear can still get him by the throat.

*The fears and hounding cares of men do not dread flashing
blades or the noise of battle. But they stalk kings and great men
and have no interest in the gleaming lure of gold*

—LUCRETIUS, *DE RERUM NATURA*, II, 47

Do fevers, migraines or gout spare him more than any of us? When the time comes that old age sits on his back, will the bowmen of his bodyguard lift it from his shoulders? When the fear of death comes upon him, can he count on the gentlemen of his bedchamber for help and comfort? When he falls prey to jealousy or other passing fancies, will doffing our hats restore his good humour? The canopy over his four-poster bed, though heavily worked with gold and pearls, has no power to ease the violence of an attack of the kidney stone:

*burning fevers do not desist more quickly if you are supine
under embroidered covers and wearing purple than if you lie
under a plebeian blanket.*

—LUCRETIUS, *DE RERUM NATURA*, II, 34

The flatterers of Alexander the Great often tried to make believe that he was the son of Jupiter. But one day he was injured and, looking at the blood oozing from the wound, he asked: 'Well? What say you now? Is this not ordinary blood, red and all too human? It is not at all the same as the blood which Homer described flowing from the wounds of gods.'

Hermodorus the poet, having written verses in honour of Antigonus in which he called him 'Son of the Sun', his master took exception to it: 'Hardly,' quoth he. 'The varlet who empties my piss-pot would tell you different.' Just so, for he is, at most, a man and though he were misshapen by an accident of birth, even being ruler of the universe could not set him to rights.

Let girls snatch him away; wherever he treads let roses grow.

—PERSIUS, *SATIRÆ*, II, 38

But what use would that be if he was coarse and witless by nature? Even the pleasures of the flesh and good fortune cannot be appreciated without vigour and understanding.

These things are like the mind that contains them: good for the mind that can make good use of them, and bad for the mind which uses them badly.

—TERENCE, *HEAUTONTIMORUMENOS*, I, III, 21

All the gifts that fortune brings, and of whatever kind they might be, require us to have a receptive soul to appreciate them. What makes us happy is enjoying them, not merely having them.

> *It was not his mansion or land, nor his mound of bronze or gold that took the fever from the sick body of their owner or removed the cares from his mind. He must be made whole again if he would enjoy his possessions. But if he is greedy or fearful, his house and estate are as painted pictures to a blind man or poultices for a gouty toe.*

—Horace, *Epistolae*, I, ii, 47

He is a fool and his taste is dull and stultified. He does not appreciate the sweetness of a Greek wine any more than a man with no palate, or as much as a horse enjoys the costly caparison with which it has been adorned. It is exactly as Plato said: health, beauty, strength and wealth and everything that is called 'good' is as bad for the unjust as it is good for the just, and vice versa for what we call 'bad'.

And if both mind and body are in a poor way, what is the use of all these external comforts, given that the slightest pinprick or some passing motion of the soul are enough to take away all the satisfaction of being sole ruler of the whole world? At the first reminder the gout gives a man of its existence, it does not help much if he is called 'Sire' or 'Your Majesty', and is surrounded *with everything made of silver and gold*

—Tibullus, *Elegiæ*, I, ii, 70

for he will surely forget all about his palaces and his greatness. If he loses his temper, will his kingly title prevent his face turning red, then pale, and prevent him gnashing his teeth like a common lunatic?

If he is a clever man and well born, a royal crown would add little to his happiness—

if your belly, lungs and feet are in good order, a king's wealth would add no more

—Horace, *Epistolae*, I, xii, 5

—for he knows that regal pomp is all puff and nonsense. Moreover he would probably share the opinion of King Seleucus, namely, that he who knows the weight of a royal sceptre would not willingly stoop down and pick it up if he were to see one lying on the ground. He said this to show how great and painful are the responsibilities incumbent on a good king. Certainly, it is no mean thing to rule others when we find it difficult to rule ourselves. Having overall command of others seems so satisfying a thing. Yet when I consider the frailty of human judgement and the difficulty of dealing with new and unfamiliar matters, I find I am strongly of the view that it is easier and much safer to follow than to lead, and that it is a great comfort to the mind to have only one beaten track to follow and answer only to oneself:

it is far better to submit and obey than seek to rule an empire.

—LUCRETIUS, *DE RERUM NATURA*, V, 1126

Add further to this what Cyrus said: no man is fit to rule who is not made of better stuff than those he would rule.

But according to Xenophon, King Hiero went further, saying that in the enjoyment of the pleasures of the flesh the great are less well placed than ordinary men, because ease and facility in obtaining them remove their bittersweet taste that we so delight in.

Too much of a love that is too strong turns tedious, just as sweet food turns the stomach

—OVID, *AMORES*, II, XIX, 25

Do we believe that choirboys find pleasure in music, or do they find it tiresome because they have too much of it? Festivities, dancing, masquerades and tournaments delight those who do not often see them but would very much like to. Yet to anyone who is accustomed to such entertainments, the taste for revels fades and loses its savour. Women cease to interest men who spend too much time enjoying them. A man who does not allow himself time to become thirsty can never truly enjoy drinking. The farces we see delight us, but they are merely chores to the players who perform them. If you wish for proof of this, Kings are much diverted—it is a holiday to them—when on occasion they don a disguise, and go among the common people *incognito* and adopt their coarse way of living.

A change is often welcomed by kings, and a plain and frugal meal under a poor man's roof, without tapestries and pomp of purple, smooths a furrowed brow.

—HORACE, *ODES*, III, XXIX, 13

Nothing is more constraining and nothing more demoralizing than abundance. What appetite, however great, would not shrivel to have three hundred women at its disposal, as the Grand Turk has in his *seraglio*? And among his ancestors, what kind of hunting and what appetite for it were shown by that lover of the chase who never went out into the fields with fewer than seven thousand falconers?

Furthermore, I do believe that the aura of grandeur casts no trivial or trifling pall over the enjoyment of the sweetest delights: the pleasures of the Great are too visible and too much in the public view.

Nor do I know how it comes about that we expect more of great personages in the way of hiding and covering up their sins. For what in us is mere indiscretion is seen in the eyes of the people to be tyranny, disdain and contempt for the law. And, any taste for vice apart, it looks as if they are hoggishly inclined to add to their pleasure by disdainfully trampling public decency underfoot. In his *Gorgias*, Plato defines a tyrant as a man who has a licence in his city to do whatever he pleases. And on account of that impunity, the brazen openness of his vice and the flagrant committing of it in public are often more damaging than the vice itself. We all hate to be spied on and probed. But kings are constantly scrutinized, even down to their physical looks, their demeanour and their private thoughts, for the entire population believe it is their right and in their interest to be judges of such matters. And, naturally enough, defects are magnified according to the eminence of the person and their visibility, so that a mole or a wart on their brow may loom larger than a scar on other brows.

That is why the poets make believe that the loves of Jupiter were disguised and conducted in a variety of shapes, none of them his, and also the reason why of all the amorous intrigues that they attribute to him there is just one, if I remember aright, in which he appears in all his greatness and majesty.

But to return to Hiero. He also tells how frustrated he felt when, confined in his royal state, he was not free to move about and travel as he pleased, being a virtual prisoner within the borders of his dominions; and how in everything he did he was constantly surrounded by a large press of people. And in truth, having myself seen our own Kings sitting alone at table, besieged by so many staring, prattling spectators, I have felt more pity for them than envy. King Alphonso was wont to say that donkeys were better placed in that respect than Kings, since their owners would at least leave them free to feed at will, whereas Kings can never obtain as much from those that serve them.

Nor has it ever crossed my mind in its most fanciful moments to think that it was in any way an advantage in the life of a man of understanding to have a score of observers gathered around his *chaise percée*, or that being attended by a courtier who, though he has an income of ten thousand livres or captured Casal or defended Siena, is in any way more helpful or welcome than having one good groom well versed in the ways of the bedchamber.

The advantages and privileges of kingship are largely imaginary. Yet every degree of good fortune has about it some whiff of sovereignty. Cæsar used the word 'kinglet' for all petty Lords who were invested with the administration of law in the France of his day. In practice, however, they went pretty far towards full kingship, stopping short only of the name of king. If we take the case of remote provinces far from the Court—let Brittany be an example—we take note of the retinue, vassals, officials, employments, functions and ceremonial practices surrounding a Lord who lives withdrawn in his own house where he is attended by his own subjects. And see to where his imagination will carry him: there is nothing more royal. He may hear some mention of his liege lord once in a year, but only as he might catch a stray allusion to the King of Persia, and will acknowledge him only on account of some distant family tie recorded as an entry in a register kept by his secretary. For it is true that our laws have a fairly light touch: the full weight of sovereignty is felt by a gentleman of France scarce twice in his lifetime. In practice, our inescapable submission as subjects in a monarchy is a concern only to those who choose to observe it because they run after honours and wealth bestowed for undertaking this or that service. For the man who prefers to sit quietly by his fireside, manages his household in peace and avoids all process of law, is effectually as free as the Doge of Venice.

Servitude enslaves few, but many are slaves to servitude.

—SENECA, *EPISTOLÆ*, XXII, 11

But most of all, Hiero insists on how deprived he feels of friendship and mutual companionship, which are the sweetest and most perfect fruits of all human existence:

'For what proof (says he) of true affection and good will can I hope to receive from the man who already owes me, whether he likes it or not, everything that is his to give? How can I ever be assured of the sincerity of his humble speech, his courtesy and his respect when the plain fact is that such things are not in his power to withhold? The honour we receive from those who fear us is not honour. Their respect is what they are obliged to show to monarchy, not to me.

The great advantage of kingship is that the people must not only do what their king tells them to, but they must also laud it to the skies.

—SENECA, *THYESTES*, II, 1, 30

'Do I not see quite clearly that a good king and a bad king, the one who is loved and the one who is loathed, have an equal amount of veneration shown to them, as much to one as to the other? The same outward display and the same ceremonial rituals were given to my predecessor and will be offered to him who succeeds me. If my subjects do nothing to anger me, it is not proof that they have any real affection for me. Why should I interpret it as such, since they could not behave otherwise even if they wanted to? None of them would follow me on account of any friendship there might be between us because there can be no friendship where there is no closeness or mutuality. My high state has removed me from relationships with men, there being too great a disparity and disproportion between us. They follow me as a matter of course, by established convention, or rather they follow my fortune in hopes of increasing their own. Everything they say to me and do for me is formal show. Their freedom is restricted on all sides by the great power I have over them and I can see nothing around me but what is posturing and affectation.'

One day, the courtiers of the Emperor Julian were applauding him for the even-handed justice he dispensed. 'I would gladly take pride in your praise,' he said, 'if it came from persons bold enough to decry or disparage actions of mine that were unjust.'

All the real enjoyments of kings are pleasures they have in common with men of middling fortunes: it is the gods who ride winged horses and dine on ambrosia. Kings have no other sleep nor other appetite than we have. Their steel is not better tempered than that with which we are armed. And their crowns do not shelter them from the sun and the rain. Diocletian, who wore a crown that was highly revered and much blessed by Fortune, renounced it to lead a quiet and private life. And when, some time afterwards, a crisis in public affairs called out for him to return and take up the burden once more, this was the answer he gave to those who had come to persuade him: 'You would not try to tempt me to it if you saw how very well the trees that I planted myself prosper in my orchard, and the fine melons I have grown from seed.'

It was the opinion of Anarcharsis that the most auspicious form of governance in a state would be—all things being equal—that in which honour and authority would be determined by men's practice of virtue and their repudiation of vice.

When King Pyrrhus resolved to lead his army into Italy, his trusty counsellor Cyneas, in an attempt to make him understand the folly of his ambition, said to him:

'Well now, Your Majesty, what is your purpose in mounting so large a venture?'

'Why, to make myself master of all Italy,' the king replied at once.

'And then,' said Cyneas, 'when that is done?'

'I shall move on to Gaul and then Spain.'

'And after that?'

'I shall sail to Africa and subdue it and then, when I have the whole world answering to me, I shall rest and live happily and without worries.'

'Then for the love of God, Sire,' returned Cyneas, 'if that is what you want, tell me what is preventing you from doing it today? Why not settle into a house in the kind of place you say you would like to live in and save yourself all the trouble and danger you put between your goal and achieving it?'

Indeed, it is because he does not know what limits to set on his desire, nor where true pleasure may lie

—Lucretius, *De Rerum Natura*, V, 1431

I shall conclude these remarks by quoting this ancient line taken from the *Life of Atticus,* by Cornelius Nepos, which I find singularly apposite and fit for my purpose:

A man's moral character is his fate.

14

On Sleep

Reason requires us always to move in the same direction, though not always at the same speed. But whereas a wise man should never permit human passions to make him stray from the straight and narrow path, he may nevertheless, without breaching his duty, allow them to lengthen or shorten his step rather than let himself stop and stand still in his road like some insensate Colossus. If Virtue were to become a living statue, I believe its pulse would beat faster going into battle than going into dinner: even virtue needs to warm up and catch fire. In this context, I have become aware of a thing quite out of the ordinary: great men who are engaged in enterprises and affairs of high consequence can sometimes remain so entirely self-possessed that not even their sleep is interrupted.

Alexander the Great, on the day appointed for his crucial battle against Darius, slept so deeply and so late in the morning that Parmenion was obliged to enter his chamber and, approaching his bedside, to call him two or three times by his name to wake him, for the hour when he should sally forth to do battle was almost on him.

The Emperor Otho, having decided to kill himself during the coming night, put his domestic affairs in order, shared out his money among his companions and sharpened the blade of the sword on which he proposed to fall, then, waiting only to learn if each and every one of his friends had retired to safety, suddenly fell so soundly asleep that the gentlemen of his chamber could hear him snoring.

The death of this emperor has much in common with that of the great Cato, even down to this detail: Cato, having readied himself for self-immolation while he waited for news to be brought of whether the senators whom he had ordered to withdraw had in fact sailed out of the port of Utica, fell into a sleep so deep that he could be heard breathing from the next room. And when the man he had sent to the port woke him to tell him that stormy weather had prevented the senators from putting to sea safely, he despatched another messenger and, settling himself down in his bed, he slept again until this second man was able to confirm that they were gone.

We may also compare his conduct with that of Alexander when, at the time of the Catiline Conspiracy, he was threatened by a great and dangerous storm in the wake of the sedition of the tribune Metellus, who was resolved to publish a decree for the recall of Pompey with his army to the city. Cato was alone in opposing the decree, and Metellus and he had exchanged angry words and dire threats in the Senate. But it was not until the next morning, in the forecourt, that the issue would be decided. There Metellus, who had the support of the people and of Cæsar—then conspiring with Pompey's party—was expected to appear. He came backed by a large cohort of foreign mercenaries and gladiators while Cato arrived fortified only with steadfastness, so that his relatives, his friends and many good and worthy people were sorely afraid for him. Some of them had spent the night together neither sleeping nor eating nor drinking on account of the danger they saw hanging over him. His wife and sisters had done nothing but weep and wail in his house, whereas he moved calmly among his supporters and comforted them. Then after supping as was his wont, he had taken himself off to bed and slept soundly until the morning when one of his fellow tribunes came to wake him for the fray. The knowledge we have of this man's great courage from the facts of his life fully justifies us in saying that it stemmed from a soul so long raised above mere events that he refused to attach any more importance to this particular business than to any other petty accident of life.

Just before the naval battle which brought Augustus victory over Sextus Pompeius in Sicily, when he was about to go forth to fight, he sank into such a deep sleep that his friends were compelled to wake him so that he might give the signal for hostilities to begin. This later gave Mark Antony the opportunity to reprove him for not having had courage enough to open his eyes wide to scan the order of his fleet and for not having shown himself to his men until Agrippa arrived with news of the victory he had gained over his enemies.

But as to the young Marius, his case was much worse, for on the day of his final battle against Sylla, after he had settled the order and disposition of his army and given the word and signal for battle, he had laid himself down in the shade of a tree to rest and fell so fast asleep that the rout and flight of his soldiers—for he had seen nothing of the fighting—were not enough to wake him. They say that it was because he had utterly worn himself out with his labours and this, together with lack of sleep, meant that nature had been able to hold out no longer.

In the light of all this, it must be left to the doctors to determine whether sleep is so necessary that our very lives depend on it. For we certainly find that King Perseus of Macedonia, being a prisoner in Rome, was put to death by being prevented from sleeping. Still, Pliny alleges that there have been those who have lived long lives without any sleep at all. We read in Herodotus of nations of men who are asleep and awake by turns in half years. And those who have written the life of the wise Epimenides agreed that he slept for fifty-seven years together.

15

On Our Lease of Life

I do not agree with the way we define our allotted lifespan. I observe that, contrary to general practice, philosophers tend to shorten theirs considerably. 'What,' said Cato the Younger to those who tried to stop him committing suicide, 'am I still of an age when you can tell me I am wrong to wish to end my life too soon?' Yes—though he was then only forty-eight. He reckoned, given how few men ever lived that long, that it was a full, even ripe old age. Those who speak of some 'life cycle' or other which they say is 'natural' and believe it may give them a few extra years may well be right—but only if they are sufficiently favoured to be spared many of the ills which, by the nature of things, befall each of us and can upset that 'cycle' on which their hopes are based.

It is an idle fancy to expect to die of the frailty which comes with extreme old age and, even more so, to assume that this is how our life will end, when it is the rarest and least likely cause of death. It is the only form of dying that we call natural, as if it were unnatural to see a man break his neck in a fall, drown in a shipwreck, succumb to plague or pleurisy; as if just being alive did not expose us to such threats. Let us not delude ourselves by using such fine words. We should instead call 'natural' those things which are general, common and universal. Dying of old age is a rare, particular, exceptional form of death and therefore very much less natural than all the other kinds—it is the last and most infrequent kind. And the further the prospect of it is from us, the smaller our chances of achieving it. Death is a bourne beyond which we shall not go, a frontier which the law of nature has ruled shall never be crossed—and it is a rare privilege to be allowed to last that long. It is an exemption which nature offers by special favour only once over the space of two or three centuries to a single individual who is freed from the obstacles and difficulties she has strewn across life's path during so many passing years.

I therefore take the view that we should consider whatever age we have reached to be one which few people ever reach. Since in the ordinary way of things men do not get that far, it is an indication that we are getting on in years. And since, too, we have exceeded the usual limits which are the true measure of our lease of life, we cannot hope to continue on much beyond them. Having many times escaped mortal perils to which we see others fall victim, we must acknowledge that such extraordinary good fortune which has brought us this far so exceeds the common expectation that it cannot possibly last much longer.

It is because our basic statutes are flawed that this false idea came about. Our laws refuse to accept that a man can manage his affairs until he is twenty-five—yet it is a matter of chance if he can manage to make his life last that long. Augustus lopped five years off Rome's ancient ordinances, declaring that thirty was a sufficient age for judges presiding over courts of law. Servius Tullius exempted knights over the age of forty-seven from active military service: Augustus lowered it to forty-five. Actually, the idea of packing men off to their homes before they are fifty-five or sixty does not seem very sensible to me. I would much prefer to see our vocations and period of service extended as much as possible for the public good. For I blame the opposite tendency which does not set our hand to the plough soon enough. That same Augustus whose judgements ruled the entire world when he was but nineteen insisted that a man be thirty before being fit to settle a dispute about the placing of a gutter on a roof.

I myself believe that our characters are as fully developed at twenty as they ever will be and that they already have the potential to do everything at that age that they are capable of achieving. No temperament which had not shown clear promise of its capabilities by then ever went on subsequently to prove its worth. Its natural qualities and powers will reveal how vigorous and fine they are within that time or never will. As they say in the Dauphiné:

> *If a thorn pricks not the day it first shows on the stem,*
> *it will scarce ever prick at all.*

Of all the glorious deeds of men committed in ancient times and our own, of each and every kind that have come to my attention, I reckon it would take me longer to list those performed by men before the age of thirty than after—yes, and often they were actions committed more than once in the lives of those same men. I quote here, without fear of contradiction, the feat of Hannibal and his great opponent Scipio.

The better half of their life was lived in the glow of fame acquired in the days of their youth and they became great men compared to others, but not so great when compared to their former selves. I myself know for certain that since I was that age, both my mind and body have gone down rather than up, backwards not forwards. It is possible that, in the case of men who make good use of their time, knowledge and experience increase with age. But vitality, quickness, toughness and other qualities more specific to us which are personally more important and crucial, dwindle and decline.

When the body is shaken by the ravages of age, blood and vigour ebb away, our wits dim, the tongue falters, the mind wanders.

—LUCRETIUS, *DE RERUM NATURA*, III, 452

Mostly it is the body that succumbs to old age, but sometimes it can be the mind. I have seen plenty of examples of men whose brains have stopped working before their stomachs or legs. And it is much more of a mortal danger because old age is not in itself a painful condition and sufferers are less aware of its symptoms, which are less acute.

On Our Lease of Life

It is for these reasons that I disagree with our laws, not because they let us labour on for too long but because they wait too long to let us begin labouring. It seems to me that, given the precariousness of life and the many perils to which it is exposed, far less emphasis should be laid on infancy, leisure and the preparation for adult life.

On Carriages

It is not difficult to demonstrate that great authors, when they write about the causes of things, do not necessarily give only the causes which they believe are true but others too, which they do not think are true but may be new or plausible in some way. What they say may be more ingenious than true and useful. So, being unsure of knowing the real cause of something, we come up with any number of others in the hope of finding it among them:

> *When a single cause is not enough, we must give many—though only one of them is true.*
>
> —LUCRETIUS, *DE RERUM NATURA*, VI, 704

You ask me: what is the origin of the custom of saying 'bless you' to anyone who sneezes? Well, we expel three sorts of air: the kind which escapes our nether parts is foul, the kind which emerges through the mouth carries a hint of rebuke for our gluttony, and the third sort is the sneeze which, because it emanates from the head and is therefore blameless, we greet with this respectful salute.

Now, you must not laugh at such subtle reasoning: it was, by repute, Aristotle who said it.

I seem to have read in Plutarch (who, of all the authors I know, is the one who best combined art and nature and judgement with knowledge), when he was explaining the cause of the sickness of the stomach which afflicts people who travel by sea, that it is caused by fear: he had already found some other evidence which proved that fear can produce such an effect. Speaking for myself, who am extremely prone to seasickness, I am quite certain that this explanation does not apply to me, and this I do not know by conjecture but by the requisite experience. Without quoting what I have been told, namely that it is something that often happens in animals, especially pigs, which have no concept of danger, plus what a friend of mine told me of his experience, that despite being very vulnerable to it, on two or three occasions while very frightened in great storms, the urge to vomit passed off, as happened to the man in ancient times—

I was too harassed for the thought of danger to enter my head.

—SENECA, *EPISTOLÆ*, LVIII, 2

I can say I have never been afraid in a boat, or anywhere else for that matter (though there have been many close calls, including the prospect of death), to a point where I was stunned or left witless. Fear can spring from errors of judgement as it can from faintness of heart. All the dangers I have lived through I saw with my eyes wide open, with my mind free, clear and undivided. But it also takes courage to be afraid. Mine once served me well when I had to beat a retreat and was able to direct and manage my escape in an orderly way which, compared with others, was, if not entirely free of trepidation, then without fear and dread. It was a tense time but not a time of hysteria and panic.

Great men go much further and describe their remarkable escapes as not merely orderly and measured but lofty and defiant. Let us remember what Alcibiades tells of the retreat of Socrates, his companion in arms: 'I found him (he says) after the rout of our army, he and Luchez bringing up the rear of those who fled. I had plenty of time to watch him in safety for I was on a good horse and he was on foot, which was how we both had fought. The first thing I noticed was how alert and determined he was, compared with Luchez, and then the boldness of his stride which was no different from his normal gait; his firm, steady cast of eye which took in and evaluated what was going on around him, looking from one group of men to another, some friends and others foes, in a way that encouraged the first and informed the rest that he would make any who tried to take his life pay dear. In this manner did they escape, because no one wanted to attack their like, preferring to chase down the frightened ones.' There you have the word of a great captain who teaches us what we may observe daily, namely, that there is nothing more likely to lead us into danger than an immoderate urge to avoid it.

Ordinarily, the less you feel the fear, the smaller feels the danger.

—LIVY, HISTORY OF ROME, XXII, v

People are wrong to say that this or that man fears death when what they mean is that he thinks much about it and foresees its coming. Foresight works equally on what concerns us for good or for ill. Reflecting on and evaluating danger can be the opposite of being frightened by it.

I do not feel I am strong enough to deal with the onset and uncontrolled violence of fear, nor indeed with any other kind of passion that disorders the mind. If I were to be felled and laid low by it, I should never get up and never be entirely the same again. Any man who made my very soul lose its footing could never set it to rights again. It could check and inspect itself for damage as nervously and carefully as it liked but it would never allow the wound it left to close up again and heal. I am fortunate that no malady has yet put my soul out of sorts. Whenever some ordeal threatens, I stand up and resist with everything I have, which means that the first onslaught that puts great pressure on me would leave me with nothing in reserve. There would be no second chances. Should my defensive dyke be breached at any point I would be helpless and drown. Epicurus says that a wise man can never change and become the opposite of wise. I have grounds for taking issue with that maxim, believing that whoever has been a fool once will never be very wise again.

God, who measures out the cold he sends according to the thickness of my clothes, also gives me passions proportionate to my ability to deal with them. Nature, having exposed me on one flank, covers me on the other and, having disabled my courage by force, arms me with a tougher skin and a level of fear that is manageable or blunted.

But I cannot put up for long (and when I was younger I found them even harder to bear) with carriages or coaches or litters or boats and now detest all forms of travel except by horse, both in town and country. I tolerate litters less than carriages and, for the same reason, prefer a good buffeting at sea that generates fear to the kind of motion you get when the weather is calm. When I feel the gentle thrusts of the oars pulling the boat under us I feel—and I could not for the life of me say how—my head spin and my stomach turn, just as they do when I sit on a rickety chair. But when sail or current carries us along or we are being towed, the steady motion does not bother me at all: it is the jerking and jouncing that upset me, especially when it is long and drawn-out. I'm not sure how I could describe my reaction any more clearly. To prevent it happening, the doctors say that I should be swaddled and tie a towel tight around my belly to hold it in. I have not tried this, for my way is to battle any ailments I might have and overcome them myself.

If my memory were sufficiently well stocked, I would not think it a waste of time to catalogue the infinite variety of ways, set out in the history books, in which carriages of diverse descriptions have been used in warfare, nation by nation, century by century, in ways which seem to me most effective, even indispensable. So much so that it is astonishing that we have forgotten everything that we once knew about them. All I will say is that quite recently, in the time of our fathers, the Hungarians made very good use of them in their undertaking against the Turks. In each of their chariots there were a shield-bearer, a musketeer and a number of harquebuses in a row ready, primed and loaded. Along the sides was a line of shields after the manner of a galiot. They faced the enemy with three thousand such chariots and, after the cannons had done their work, they either ordered the charioteers to fire on the enemy, who were forced to swallow their salvos as a foretaste of what was to come (which was no small mouthful), or they launched them at the enemy's squadrons to scatter them and cut a way through, or used them to protect the flanks of their troops against ambush as they marched through open terrain, or to defend an encampment and fortify it at speed. In my day, a gentleman of portly figure stationed on one of our frontiers was unable to find a horse that would bear his weight. But having made enemies there, he took to travelling around the country in a chariot not unlike those I have described, and managed very well. But that is quite enough about chariots of war.

The Kings of our founding [Merovingian] dynasty went everywhere in carts drawn by four oxen. Mark Antony was the first to be driven into Rome—with a minstrel wench at his side—in a carriage drawn by lions. Later, Heliogabalus did the same, styling himself Cybele, mother of the gods, but he also used tigers when pretending to be the god Bacchus. He once harnessed a pair of stags to his carriage and another time four dogs, and even four nude women, and was pulled along by them in great style, himself also being naked. The emperor Firmus also rode in a carriage, but one drawn by ostriches of such astounding size that he seemed to be flying and not trundling along. Such strange and fanciful antics prompt a thought, namely, that trying so hard to draw attention to themselves and make an impression with excessive expenditure are in monarchs signs of a lack of confidence and evidence that they are insufficiently sure of their position. This might be understandable when they are abroad, but not among their own subjects, where their power is unlimited and the dignity of their kingship is the highest degree of honour they can attain. Likewise, I do not think it necessary for a gentleman to dress up when he is at home: his residence, his style of life and his table speak for him.

There seem to me to be good, sensible, rational grounds for the advice which Isocrates gave his king: 'That the furnishings of his house and the plate of his table should be magnificent, for they represent expenditure of lasting value and will be inherited by those who come after him; but that he should avoid ostentatious display which quickly fades both as show and in the memory.'

When I was young, in the absence of honours and distinctions, I revelled in fine clothes and looked well in them: but there are people on whom fine clothes droop and look sad.

We have records that show the amazing tight-fistedness of kings in the matter of personal appearance and grants bestowed—and they were great kings possessed of high reputations, wealth and good fortune. Demosthenes railed bitterly against the laws of his city, which allocated public monies specifically for lavish displays of games and festivals. He wanted its civic greatness to be shown rather by the number of its sea-worthy ships and well-equipped armies. And there is good reason to censure Theophrastus who, in his book *On Riches*, set out a contrary position, maintaining that the nature of such expenditure is a proper product of opulence. But, says Aristotle, those pleasures impress only the most vulgar of the common people and, once they have wearied of them, fade quickly from their memory. No man of sober judgement can have any regard for them whatsoever.

To me, the money would be more in keeping with majesty, more useful and have more lasting benefits if spent on financing ports and harbours, fortifications and ramparts, elegant buildings, churches, hospitals, schools and on the improvement of streets and high roads. By doing just that in my lifetime, Pope Gregory XIII has left a very favourable legacy, and in the same vein our own Queen Catherine [de Medici] would be remembered for years to come for maintaining her natural generosity and munificence if her means were able to match her caring attentiveness. Fortune has greatly irked me by interrupting the building of the Pont-Neuf, such a beautiful bridge, in our great city, thus ruling out any hope of my ever seeing it in use before I die.

On top of all that, to a monarch's subjects, who are the spectators of these extravagant displays, it seems that it is their wealth that is on liberal show and that they are being entertained at their own expense. Their subjects naturally believe of their Kings what we believe of our servants, namely, that their function is to ensure they supply us plentifully with whatever we need but that they cannot assume that they are entitled to any part of the money for their own personal use. Yet the Emperor Galba, having enjoyed hearing a musician perform while he supped, ordered his treasure chest to be brought, rummaged in it and put into the man's hand a fistful of crowns, saying: 'This is not public money but mine own.' But more often than not, it turns out that the people are right: they are given feasts for their eyes not food for their bellies.

Generosity itself does not appear in the best light when shown by kings. Private persons have a better claim to be thought generous because, strictly speaking, a king owns nothing and owes even his person to all.

Court sentences are not handed down in the interest of the judge but in the best interests of those who appear before him. Our superiors are appointed not for their own good, but for that of those subservient to them, and similarly doctors are employed to help the sick and not themselves. The purpose of all forms of public office, as of all crafts and skills, is always greater than the private interest of their holder. As Cicero says: 'no art looks only to itself'.

This is why the tutors of princes make a point of instilling into their young charges that there is virtue in extravagance. They drum it into them that they should never refuse any request and that the best use of money is to give it away (a lesson which I recall has been much honoured during my own lifetime). But such instructors are either more concerned with their own interest than with that of their master, or else do not understand their duties given whom it is they are instructing. Now, it is all too easy to instil liberality in someone who has the wherewithal to be as generous as he pleases with someone else's money. And because munificence is not judged by the size of a gift but by the wealth of the giver, it becomes meaningless when it flows from such powerful hands. Such donors are prodigal, not liberal. Such lavishness is not one of the most commendable of kingly virtues and is the only one, according to Dionysius the Tyrant, that is compatible with tyranny. So I should prefer to teach my pupil this verse [cited by Plutarch] by an ancient Greek ploughman:

For a good crop a man must sow the seed by hand,
not pour it straight from the sack.

The seed must be properly broadcast not carelessly scattered. Before giving, or more accurately, paying back and recompensing so many people for services rendered, a king must be a fair and even-handed distributor of rewards. If the liberality of a king is unselective and indiscriminate, I would much rather he was a pinchpenny.

Royal virtue seems to lie primarily in justice, and of all the branches of justice, it is the kind shown in the exercise of liberality that best characterizes kings, for they have specifically tended to make it an area for which they are personally responsible: all other forms of justice they exercise through intermediaries. Immoderate largesse is a poor way of acquiring goodwill since it alienates more people than it charms;

The more help you have given, the less you can give. Now, what greater folly is there than making what you like to do impossible to go on doing?

—CICERO, *DE OFFICIIS*, II, 15

And if largesse is given without reference to merit, it is an embarrassment to him who receives it, and he will receive it without gratitude. Tyrants have been sacrificed to the hatred of the people by the actions of men they themselves had raised on high; the kind of men who think they can consolidate their possession of ill-gotten goods and property by displaying their contempt and loathing for the very man from whom they received their booty. And so they turn their coats and switch their loyalties in order to acquire the favourable judgement and general good opinion of the people.

The subjects of a king who is extravagant in his spending will themselves turn excessive in their demands. They will cut their coats not according to reason but by his example. There are certainly occasions when we should blush at our effrontery. For by any standard of equity we are overpaid when the reward we receive equals the service we have rendered, for we owe our king nothing except what is required by our natural obligation to thrones. If he pays the bill for the expenses we incur, he does too much; it is enough that he should contribute a portion of the cost. Any more amounts to a bonus, and bonuses cannot be demanded, for does not the word liberality have an echo in it of liberty and imply 'freely given'? But in our way of doing things, there is no end to it. What has been received does not count and we look only to what more we shall receive in future. Which is why the more a king gives in largesse, the fewer the friends that will remain to him. How can he meet all the demands which continue to grow even as he satisfies them? The man who has his mind on receiving does not think about what he has already received. The essence of greed is ingratitude.

The example of Cyrus is not out of place here as a pointer to Kings in our own age for helping them to know whether their largesse is well or badly bestowed. It would also enable them to see how much better that emperor fared than they in this regard, and how in the end they are always reduced, by their lavish giving, to having to borrow from subjects they do not know, indeed more often from those whom they have treated ill than from those whom they have treated well and from whom they receive 'gifts' which are free only in name. Crœsus took Cyrus to task for his largesse and calculated how his exchequer would have stood if he had been less open-handed. Cyrus sought to justify his generosity and so sent out letters to the great and good in all parts of his

dominions, especially to those he had most particularly bene-
fited, begging them to come to his help in his time of need by
donating whatever they could afford and to send him a note
of the amount. When all the responses were in, it transpired
that each of his friends, not thinking it was enough to offer
him only the equivalent of what they had received in royal
largesse, had added a significant sum of their own money. It
turned out that the total received came to far more than the
amount of the savings Crœsus had calculated. Whereupon
Cyrus said to him: 'I am no less interested in money than other
monarchs but I am in fact rather more careful in looking after
it. You can see how, for so small an outlay of effort, I have
come by an incalculable fortune from my many friends and
how much better they are as ministers of finance than any
number of mercenary men who have no obligation to nor
affection for me; my money is safer with them than in my
vaults where it would attract hatred, envy and the contempt
of other monarchs.'

Roman Emperors would defend the sheer number of
games and public spectacles they financed by saying that their
authority rested (at least outwardly) on the will of the Roman
people who, from time immemorial, had been accustomed to
being wooed by such entertainments and excesses. In reality
it was mainly private individuals who, using their own money,
had encouraged this habit of gratifying their fellow citizens
and compatriots with such profusion and extravagance. But
the character of this custom changed when those who became
the masters chose to imitate it:

On Carriages

*Giving money taken from its rightful owners to strangers should
not be seen as liberality*

—CICERO, *DE OFFICIIS*, I, 14

Phillip, because his son had attempted to win over the
Macedonians to his side by using gifts, rebuked him in a letter
which began: 'Come now, is it your intention that your subjects should regard you as their bursar and not as their king?
If you want to keep them loyal, then do so with virtuous acts
and not with your money-bags.'

Yet it was a fine thing to have done, to think of planting in
and around the amphitheatre a great number of large trees
with spreading branches in full leaf which impersonated a
shady forest set out in symmetrical order and in it, on the
first day, to have released a thousand each of ostriches, boars
and deer and then to allow them to be hunted by the people;
on the second day to have arranged, in their presence, for the
killing of a hundred great lions, a hundred leopards and three
hundred bears; on the third day to have three hundred pairs
of gladiators fight to the death, as the Emperor Probus did. It
was an equally fine thing to view those great arenas dressed on
the outside with marble and embellished with various figures
and statues and, on the inside, decorated with different kinds
of rare and glittering ornamental features—

*see here the arcade like a jewelled baldric, and there a gilded
portico*

—CALPURNIUS, *ECLOGUES*, VII, 47

—and also to see every slope of that great empty space filled and tiered from top to bottom with sixty or eighty terraced rows of seats, also marble, and provided with cushions—

They'll say, 'You should be ashamed! You can't sit there if you can't afford to. Those seats are reserved for knights only'

—JUVENAL, SATIRÆ, III, 153

—which could comfortably seat a hundred thousand spectators. And no less fine a sight was the way the floor of the arena, where the games took place, was first by some ingenious contrivance exposed in sections to reveal cavities simulating animal lairs from which would spring the beasts that appeared in the spectacle; second, how it was flooded to create a deep sea roiling with sea monsters and fully armed warships enacting a naval battle; thirdly, to see it drained and cleared for the combats of the gladiators; and fourthly, after spreading it not with sand but vermilion and oily resin, to stage a solemn banquet for the infinity of people there, this being the grand finale—the last act of that same day!

How often did we see parts of the arena floor sink and gape, and from the pits below emerged wild beasts and a forest of trees made golden with saffron. But not only did we see creatures of the forest: I saw bears pitted against sea-monsters and bull-calves, a deformed kind of cattle which are dignified by the name of 'sea-horses'.

—CALPURNIUS, ECLOGUES, VII, 64

Sometimes they raised a great hill, covered it with fruit trees and verdure and from the top of it installed a river of water which rushed down as from a living spring. Sometimes they sailed a great ship there that opened its sides which fell away and, after releasing four or five hundred fighting beasts from its belly, simply closed up again and vanished of its own accord. Or again, on the arena's lowest level, they made perfumed water shoot continuously into the air in jets and spouts to such a height that the numberless multitude was sprayed with fragrant dew. As protection against the fierce sun, across the entire bowl they stretched either cloths of purple embroidered with needlework or silks in different colours. It was but the work of a moment to draw them across and retract them as required.

> *The sun may be beating down on the spectators, but the awnings are always opened when [that swine] Hermogenes puts in an appearance.*

—Martial, *Epigrams*, XII, xxix, 15

Even the nets strung out in front of the spectators to protect them from the violence of the lunging beasts were woven of gold too: 'The woven nets are refulgent with gold' (Calpurnius, *Eclogues*).

If anything can justify such excesses, this was an instance where creativity and originality generated more wonderment than cost.

In these displays of vanity we can see how fertile those

times were in minds more original than ours. It is with that sort of creativity as it is with everything else that nature produces. That is not to say that in those days she was operating at her highest level. But we do not stride boldly forward; we dawdle, we try this way and then that, we take steps backwards. I fear that our learning in all areas is deficient. We can neither see very far ahead nor very far back. Our knowledge is without curiosity, a lifeless thing, being shallow and limited both in time and scope.

There were brave men before Agamemnon, but though many,
all were sent, unwept and unknown into the long night

—Horace, *Odes*, IV ix, 25

Other poets celebrated other events before the Trojan war and
the fall of Troy

—Lucretius, *De Rerum Natura*, V, 327

In this context, it seems to me that we should not dismiss the narrative of Solon, which tells what he had learnt from the priests of Egypt about the great antiquity of their nation and their manner of unearthing and preserving the histories of other nations.

If we could see the infinity of space and time, which stretches
away boundlessly in every direction, and if our mind were able
to wander through it far and wide, rushing hither and thither
without ever reaching any limit that halted its journeying, we

should discover in that vast infinity the power that moves an
infinite variety of forms.

—CICERO, *DE NATURA DEORUM*, I, xx, 54

If everything that has come down to us about the past were
true and known to some one person, it would be as nought
compared to what we do not know. And as to the very idea
that the world goes on its own sweet way while we are on it,
how puny and parochial is the knowledge of it in the most
enquiring minds! Not only of particular events which by
chance may often be revealing and significant, and of the
current state of civil governments and great nations: we miss
a hundred times more than what comes to our attention. We
hailed the invention of our artillery and the printing press as
miracles. But other men, on the other side of the world, in
China, had the use of both a thousand years before us. If we
could see as much of the world as we do not see, we would
observe, as seems very likely, a constant multiplication and
variation of created forms. There is nothing that is unique
and rare in nature. This is not the case with our knowledge,
which is not much of a foundation on which to base our
scientific laws which all too easily give us a very false picture
of things. How ineffectually do we now define the decline
and decrepitude of the world using arguments drawn from
our own inadequacies and decline: 'Our age lacks energy,
even the soil is exhausted' (Lucretius, II, 1151). The poet I
quote pronounced erroneously on the creation and youth
of our world, basing his judgement on the vigour he saw in

the minds of the men of his time which produced many new
ideas and inventions.

*It is my opinion that the entire universe is newly born, as is
the world the age of which is not remote; which is why certain
inventions are still being improved and refined, such as our
proficiency in navigation*

—LUCRETIUS, *DE RERUM NATURA*, V. 331

Our world has just discovered a new one (and who will say
if it is the last of its brothers, since until now Daemons,
Sybils and ourselves have all been unaware of its existence?)
which is no less extensive, no less populous and no less well-
proportioned than ours, yet is so new and infant-like that we
are still teaching it its ABC. Less than fifty years ago, it knew
nothing of writing or anything of weights, measures, clothes
or corn or grapevines. It was still naked on its mother's knee,
depending for its very life on its wet nurse's milk. If we are
right about the imminent ending of our world and the poet is
right that his is young, then this New World will not emerge
into the light until such time as ours is leaving it. The whole
world will become paralysed, with one half of it lame and
the other fit and strong. I feel that we will be responsible for
hastening the decline and ruin of this newcomer by our con-
tamination of it, and that we will have made it pay a heavy
price for our ideas and acquired skills. It was a child-like world.
Yet have we not whipped and forced it to submit by abusing
our power and natural strengths to make it adopt our way of

doing things? Did we treat it with our standards of justice and benevolence? Were we magnanimous in conquest? Overall, the reactions of its people and our negotiations with them show that they were in no way inferior to us in their grasp of issues and natural clarity of mind. The stunning magnificence of the cities of Cusco and Mexico and, among various others of the same ilk, the gardens of the king where all the trees, fruits and plants were arranged by kind and size as they would occur in a normal garden, but here reproduced with exquisite skill in gold, as too were all the animals born in his domains and seas, also on show in his collections. And the beauty of their artefacts of precious stones, feathers and cotton, and paintings too, reveal that they had little to learn from us in craftsmanship.

And where religion, their respect for law, their goodness, generosity, honesty and plain dealing are concerned, the fact that we had so much less of those virtues served us well, for by surrendering this advantage they were lost, sold out and betrayed—by their superiority!

As to boldness and courage, and their fortitude, commitment and resoluteness in the face of pain, hunger and death, I would not hesitate to set instances of their conduct beside the most famous examples from antiquity which we have in our memories on this side of the world. Because if we set aside the ruses and ploys used to mislead and confuse them by the men who conquered them, and the understandable bewilderment of entire peoples caused by the unexpected arrival of men who wore beards and were so very different from them in language, religion, stature and bearing; who came from a faraway part of the world where they had never dreamt there was any human habitation; strangers who rode great unknown monsters to fight a people which had never before seen a horse or any kind of beast capable of carrying and supporting a man or any other kind of weight; warriors each encased in a hard, shining hide and armed with sharp, gleaming weapons to use against men who, for the miracle of a knife or the reflection in a looking glass, would give a fortune in gold and pearls; who, even if they had had the time, possessed neither the skill nor the materials with which to discover a means of piercing cold steel; to all this add the thunder and lightning of our cannon and harquebuses, which would have unmanned Cæsar himself if, having no more experience of such things than they, he had been taken unawares by such novelties, and were now used against men who were naked (except in localities where a method had been discovered of making some kinds of cotton cloth), peoples who had no weapons other than bows, stones, staves and wooden shields, whole nations duped by professions of friendship and good faith, and wrong-footed by their curiosity to see strange and unfamiliar things—take all these advantages away from the *conquistadores*, say I, and you strip away everything that made so many victories possible.

When I think of the unquenchable fire with which so many thousands of men, women and children faced certain danger and did battle so many times in defence of their gods and their liberty, and showed such selfless determination to suffer extreme hardship, violence and death rather than submit to the power of those by whom they were so shamefully ill-used... and when I reflect on those who were imprisoned and preferred to let themselves die lingeringly of hunger than be fed by the hand of enemies so odiously victorious—at such moments I am certain that no matter who they had fought on a level field with equal weapons, experience and numbers, they would have been as dangerous, nay, more, as in any war that we see fought today.

Why was it not given to Alexander or the ancient Greeks and Romans to make of this invasion an honourable and noble conquest? Why was not such a great change and the transformation of so many empires and nations brought about by more civilized hands, which would have gently smoothed and tamed what was rough and wild while fostering the seeds which nature had already sown by promoting through the cultivation of the land and the beautification of cities the spread of arts and crafts as and when they were needed, but also gradually infusing their established values with Greek and Roman virtues? The whole world might have been steered onto a new path and the entire enterprise redeemed if the first examples of our conduct in those regions had inspired admiration and the will to imitate virtue, and built between them and us fraternal relations and understanding! How easy it would have been to train up such unspoilt souls, all eager to learn and for the most part generously endowed by nature!

Instead of which we exploited their ignorance and inexperience to shepherd them more easily towards treachery, lust, avarice and all types of inhumanity and cruelty, by the model and example of our ways. Whoever set such great store by commerce and trade? And the cost? Cities razed to the ground, whole nations exterminated, many millions of people put to the sword and the finest and richest part of the world turned upside down by wrangles about the price of pearls and pepper! Ah! The victory of the money-men! Never did ambition, never did the conflicts of public life set men against each other and result in such unspeakable bloodshed and pitiful disasters!

Sailing along the coast searching for the natives' gold mines, Spaniards landed in a fertile region, pleasing to the eye and with a large population. They began with their usual cautionary patter. They came (they said) in peace, after a long voyage across the sea, being sent by the King of Castille, the greatest king of the inhabited world, to whom the Pope— God's representative on earth—had granted the principality of all the Indies. And that if they consented to pay tribute to him, they would be treated with great kindness. They asked for food to eat and the gold they said they needed to prepare medicines. Furthermore, they sternly pressed on them their belief in one God and the truth of our religion which they advised them—with menaces—to embrace.

The response was as follows: that, as for coming in peace, then if they truly did, they did not look very peaceful. As to their king and what he asked for, then he must be poor indeed to come begging and scarcely have a shoe to his foot. As to the man who had given him such dominions, he was clearly a lover of strife if he was prepared to give to a third party that which was not his to give and thus set him at odds with those who had owned it from time immemorial. As to provisions, these they would supply but of gold they had but little, adding that it was a thing they did not value highly, since it was of little practical use in their lives which they devoted entirely to living happily and agreeably. But the strangers were free to have whatever gold they could find, except for that used in the service of their gods. As to there being only one God, they had liked the homily well enough, but had no wish to change their religion, having become profitably accustomed to practise it for so long a time. They said too they were in the habit of seeking advice only from their friends and acquaintances. As for the threats offered, it was a sign of poor judgement to go about threatening peoples of whose character and power they knew nothing. So they should pack up at once and remove themselves from their territory, for it was not their habit to take in good part such uncivil courtesies and warnings from strangers armed head to foot. If not, they would be dealt with as they had dealt with others of their kind.

At which point they referred them to the heads displayed on their city walls of men executed according to their laws.

And there you have an example for the so-called prattle of these 'children'!

But as it happened, although other material items were available there, it is clear that in that particular place as elsewhere the Spaniards did not find the goods they were looking for, nor did they tarry there or attempt any sort of search for other treasures there might have been in that place: on this, see my essay on Cannibals.

Of the two most powerful monarchs in that New World (and maybe also of this), Kings of many Kings, the last to be unseated, one, the King of Peru, was captured in battle and held for such an excessive ransom that it beggars belief. After he had straightforwardly paid the sum, he had given by the manner of his conversation a clear indication of being a man of candid, liberal and sterling character and clear and quick understanding. His captors took it into their heads—after first extracting one million, three hundred and twenty-five thousand five hundred ounces of gold, not to mention silver and other riches which amounted to as much again and more, so that their horses were actually shod with solid gold—to wonder, thinking nought of the dishonesty of their intentions, what other treasures the king might possess that he had held back, which they might now get their hands on. They made a false charge against him and showed evidence that he was guilty of conspiring to raise the provinces to rebellion to set him free. Next, by a canting decision of the court fabricated by the same men who had worked this treachery against him, he was sentenced to be publicly hanged and strangled, having first been forced to buy an absolution that spared him the agony of being burned alive by accepting baptism, which was administered immediately prior to his execution. It was a horrifying, unexampled torment which, however, he endured without demeaning either by look or word the dignity and gravity of royalty. Then, to calm the people who were dumbfounded and numbed to see a thing so unheard-of, a great show of mourning for his death was staged, followed by a sumptuous interment.

The other monarch, the King of Mexico, having at length defended his besieged city and demonstrated—if ever a king and his people did—what suffering and endurance can achieve, it was his misfortune to be delivered alive into the hands of his enemies, his capitulation being on the understanding that he would be treated like a king (nor in prison did he do anything that was unworthy of that dignity). When after their victory the Spaniards had failed to find as much gold as they had expected, they ransacked the city and hunted high and low. They then set about extracting information by subjecting their prisoners to the most excruciating forms of torture that they could devise. But unable to get answers from men whose courage proved stronger than their sufferings, they eventually grew so enraged that, riding roughshod over their honour and the law of nations, they sentenced the king together with one of his principal courtiers to be tortured, each in the presence of the other. The noble lord, overwhelmed by agony and encircled by burning braziers, finally looked up pitifully towards his master, as if to ask his forgiveness because he could endure no more. The king turned sternly and rested his proud gaze on him to upbraid him for being a coward and afraid, but said only these words in a steady, cracked voice: 'And what of me? Am I in my bath? Am I any more comfortable than you?' Moments later, the man succumbed to his agony and died where he lay. The king, half burnt alive, was removed from the place, but not for pity's sake (for what compassion could there be in the hearts of men who in return for dubious information about some gold object that they could steal, were prepared to roast a man and stand by and watch, not just a man, but a king so great in destiny and merit?) but because his resistance made their cruelty seem all the more shameful. Later, for having bravely attempted by force of arms to liberate himself from his long captivity and bondage, they hanged him. He died a death that well became so magnanimous a prince.

On another occasion, they burned alive, at the same time, four hundred and sixty men, of which four hundred were commoners and sixty were prominent lords of the province, but all plain prisoners of war. We have various accounts of it written by the Spaniards themselves, in which they not only admit what they did but boast of it and advocate the practice. Would that have been to provide a record of their practice of justice? Or as evidence of their zeal in religion? What is clear is that their ways are too contrary and too opposed to so sacred a cause. If indeed they intended to spread our faith, they might have reflected that it is not the conquest of new lands that makes it grow but the conquest of men's minds. And had they been content merely with the killing which of necessity accompanies wars, they would not also have unthinkingly committed massacres as casually they would the slaughter of wild beasts, and made them as universal as their swords and fire could make them, in furtherance of their policy of sparing only as many as they purposed to keep alive as wretched slaves to be employed to labour in their mines. As a result, a number of Conquistador captains, almost all of them fallen from grace and hated by all, were put to death at the scene of their conquests by order of the Kings of Castille who were rightly outraged by the horror of their conduct. God deservedly allowed all their vast spoils to be swallowed up as they were being transported by sea to Europe, or lost during internecine conflicts in which the rogues killed each other, most being buried where they fell and seeing no reward from all their conquering.

As for the wealth sent back to Spain and placed in the hands of a thrifty and prudent king [Phillip II], it failed to live up to the assurances given to his predecessors and fell well short of the initial influx of riches which had flowed from those new lands (for although a great deal is still brought back, we see that it is as nothing compared with how much might have been expected). The explanation for this is that the use of coinage was entirely unknown in the New World so that all the gold ended up in one place, and, being of no use except for ornament and show, it was akin to furniture to be handed down from father to son by a number of powerful Kings who continued to exhaust their mines in order to build up a great heap of plate and a quantity of statues to adorn their palaces and their temples. But with us, gold is entirely used in trade and commerce. We divide it into small pieces and cast it into many different forms; we disperse it and make it circulate. But imagine if our monarchs had similarly amassed a hoard of all the gold they could acquire over a period of centuries and thus immobilized it!

The inhabitants of the Kingdom of Mexico were somewhat more enlightened and sophisticated than those of the other nations of that region. They accordingly believed, as we do, that the universe was close to its end and took as a sign of this our manner of laying waste to their land. They believed that the life of the world was divided into five ages and a procession of five successive suns, of which the first four had already outrun their time, and that the sun which shone on them was the fifth. The first had perished, and with it all created beings, in a universal deluge of water. The second ended when the sky fell and choked every living thing: this they called the age of giants and they showed the Spaniards heaps of bones of such proportions that men of that age would have been twenty feet tall. The third perished by fire which burned and consumed everything. The fourth ended with a mighty movement of air and wind which blew everything down, even mountains; the humans did not die but were changed into baboons (there is no end to the fancies which human gullibility will swallow!); after the death of this fourth sun, the world remained in perpetual darkness for twenty-five years. During the fifteenth of these years were created a man and a woman who restarted the human race; ten years later, on a certain day, the Sun reappeared newly born; and they number their years from its birth. On the third day after its creation, the old gods died and new ones were subsequently born from time to time. My author [López de Gómara] was unable to discover how they think this last sun will die. But their dating of the fourth of the series agrees with the great conjunction of the spheres which, eight hundred or so years ago, according to the calculations of astrologers, produced profound transformations and revolutions in the world.

As to the pomp and splendour which first drew me to embark on this subject, not Greece nor Rome nor Egypt can boast any of their constructions which, in terms of practical usefulness, complexity or noble achievement, can compare with the road to be seen in Peru, built by that nation's Kings, that links the cities of Quito and Cusco—three hundred leagues of it, long, dead straight, flat, twenty-five paces wide, paved, with, to each side, high handsome walls along the foot of which run streams of water which never stop flowing, and bordered by a stately variety of trees which they call *molly*. Whenever they encountered mountains or crags, they cut through and levelled them and filled ravines with chalk and rock. At the end of each day's stage are handsome palaces well-stocked with victuals, weapons and changes of clothes both for travellers and for the armies which have occasion to pass that way.

In my assessment of this great building work, I have taken into account the degree of difficulty which is very great in that terrain. In the process of its construction, no stone blocks were used which were less than ten feet square. They had no other means of moving them except by manhandling and dragging them, and this at a time when the art of scaffolding was not known to them and consisted of piling up increments of rubble against whatever was being built and then of removing it afterwards.

But let us return to our carriages.

Instead of carriages, carts and any wheeled conveyance of that sort, they travelled only on the shoulders of bearers. It was in this fashion that the last King of Peru, on the day he was made prisoner, was carried into battle seated on a gold chair borne on poles of gold. As many men as the Spaniards hacked down to make him fall to the ground (for they wished to take him alive), the same number fought for the honour of taking the place of the dead. It was thus quite impossible to dislodge him, however many of those men were slaughtered—until a man on a horse seized the king bodily and pulled him to the ground.